Into the Story 2

Into the Story 2

More Stories! More Drama!

Carole Miller and Juliana Saxton

intellect Bristol, UK / Chicago, USA

First published in the UK in 2016 by
Intellect, The Mill, Parnall Road, Fishponds, Bristol, BS16 3JG, UK

First published in the USA in 2016 by
Intellect, The University of Chicago Press, 1427 E. 60th Street,
Chicago, IL 60637, USA

A catalogue record for this book is available from the British Library.

Copy-editor: MPS Technologies
Cover designer: Jane Seymour
Production manager: Richard Kerr
Typesetting: Contentra Technologies

Print ISBN: 978-1-78320-574-5
ePDF ISBN: 978-1-78320-575-2
ePUB ISBN: 978-1-78320-576-9

Printed and bound by Hobbs, UK

This is a peer-reviewed publication.

Permissions

The authors and publisher wish to thank those who have generously given permission to reprint borrowed material:

The Follower by Richard Thompson, Fitzhenry & Whiteside, Toronto, ON, 2000. Used by permission. From "Story Drama Structures" by Juliana Saxton and Carole Miller in *Process Drama and Multiple Literacies: Addressing Social, Cultural and Ethical Issues* edited by Jenifer Jasinski Schneider, Thomas P. Crumpler, and Theresa Rogers. Copyright Heinemann, 2006. Published by Heinemann, Portsmouth, NH. Reprinted by permission of the publisher.

From the book *Wilfrid Gordon McDonald Partridge* by Mem Fox and Julie Vivas. Text copyright Mem Fox, 1984. Illustrations copyright Julie Vivas, 1984. First published by Omnibus Books, a division of Scholastic Australia Pty Limited, 1984. Reproduced by permission of Scholastic Australia Pty Limited; Penguin Books/ Dorling Kindersley, London, England, 1987; Kane Miller Books, San Diego, CA, 1989.

Those Shoes. Text copyright Maribeth Boelts, 2007. Illustrations copyright 2007 by Noah Z. Jones. Reproduced by permission of the publisher, Candlewick Press, Somerville, MA.

Tricycle. Written by Elisa Amado, illustrated by Alfonso Ruano, copyright Stickland Ltd., 2015.

Antonio Skármeta. *La Composición*, copyright Antonio Skármeta, 1998. *The Composition*, Groundwood Books, Toronto, ON, 2000. Used by permission.

The Fish Princess by Irene Watts, Tundra Books, Toronto ON, 1996. Used by permission of the author.

"Mary Ellery", a pre-text by Norah Morgan in *Asking Better Questions* by Norah Morgan and Juliana Saxton, Pembroke, Markham ON, 2006. Used by permission.

Rose Blanche by Roberto Innocenti, The Creative Company, Mankato, MN, 1985. Used by permission.

Beneath the Surface by Gary Crew and Steven Woolman, Lothian Children's Books, an imprint of Hachette Australia, 2004.

From *Woolvs in the Sitee* by Margaret Wild. Copyright Margaret Wild, 2007. Published by Boyds Mills Press. Used by permission.

To our friends, colleagues and students around the world, where would we be without you?

Gross National Product does not allow for the health of our children, the quality of their education, or the joy of their play. It does not include the beauty of our poetry or the strength of our marriages; the intelligence of our public debate or the integrity of our public officials. It measures neither our wit nor our courage; neither our wisdom nor our learning; neither our compassion nor our devotion to our country; it measures everything, in short, except that which makes life worthwhile.

Robert F. Kennedy, 1968

Contents

Foreword

First, and on a personal note, I am at once humbled and privileged to write this foreword. Carole Miller and Juliana Saxton are for me what L. M. Montgomery's Anne Shirley described as "kindred spirits". They have generously shared their knowledge, expertise and understanding about drama, literature, language and literacy over more than two decades with me and countless others all over the world. Their presentations, workshops and writing have taught us so much. We have all learned from their scholarship, wise mentoring and professional practice.

In this long awaited sequel to their widely used *Into the Story: Language in Action through Drama* (2004), Miller and Saxton once again weave together two art forms: drama and literature, in particular contemporary picture books. The ten story drama structures provide a wealth of carefully sequenced strategies, questions and ideas that enable teachers to scaffold and nurture children's imaginative and creative potential. Such journeys into and beyond text and image foster the dispositions or habits of mind that are critical for life in the twenty-first century.

Few educators would dispute the power of stories in shaping lives and identities. Not only do we tell stories hundreds of times each day, we make sense of who we are through stories. Powerful stories can be transformational: they can change the way we think about a person or an issue or the way we live. Transformative stories are central in this book. Miller and Saxton have chosen the stories with care and these wonderful selections help us "find the best expression of the human imagination, … the most useful means by which we come to grips with our ideas about ourselves and what we are" (Chambers, 1985, p. 16).

International research increasingly underlines the important role that arts rich and creative pedagogies can and should play in developing children's affective and academic outcomes. In an important meta-analysis for the OECD for example, Winner, Goldstein, and Vincent-Lancrin (2013) examined the extent arts in education develops skills such as critical and creative thinking, self-confidence, motivation, cooperation and the ability to communicate. Their report concludes that engagement in enactment through classroom drama strengthens students' reading, writing and text understanding, enhancing empathy, perspective taking and emotion regulation (p. 8).

Enactment or walking in someone else's shoes is often regarded as the essence of classroom drama. Moving from the physical enactment or embodiment of a character or an idea or an event to a visual and then written representation strengthens our neural circuitry (Heath, 2000) and enables us to continue to build our imaginative and creative potential (e.g. Baldwin, 2012; Crumpler & Schneider, 2002; Booth & Neelands, 1998). Further, many case studies document the power of drama to change traditional classroom discourse to enable students to ask the big philosophical questions and think for themselves instead of trying to play "guess what's in the teacher's head" (e.g. Ewing, 2010; Morgan & Saxton, 2006; O'Mara, 2004; Sinclair et al., 2009). Importantly, Miller and Saxton remind us that it is only part of the story. They demonstrate that it is the whole body engagement with another that is at the heart of drama and they help us begin to meaningfully connect with others. Through dramatic play we can put our own world on hold, step into another's and behave "as if" to work through a dilemma, make sense of an experience, understand a different perspective or motivation and genuinely feel compassion for the plight of another.

Each chapter in *More Stories! More Drama!* embodies the conditions that effectively foster creative and imaginative thinking in the classroom. These conditions include:

- providing meaningful, relevant and creative learning experiences that encourage emotional connections and the development of affective empathy;
- asking "I wonder" and "what if" kinds of questions and ensuring adequate space and time for deep exploration/investigation and reflection;
- planning collaborative tasks that trigger rich conversations: enabling students to exchange ideas, disagree with each other and justify their reasons for perspectives—higher order thinking;
- encouraging the expression and representation of ideas in a range of different media;
- integrating subject areas rather than silo-ing knowledge into separate discipline slices.

Unfortunately such learning opportunities are under threat or non-existent in many contemporary classrooms. Increasingly, the rapid pace of twenty-first century lives and an ever-narrowing school curriculum means that less time and space is made available for play. Children and young people are often caught up in the complexities of adults' busy lives as well as politically driven policy demands for overly structured and transmissive programmes with academic success measured by high-stakes testing. Time for imagination and creativity is too often squeezed out. Hirsh-Pasek and Golinkoff (2003) describe this trend in the United States of America as a crisis for children in terms of their cognitive, social, spiritual, emotional and physical development.

This book is therefore timely, given it enables a different educational philosophy and pedagogy. The rich stories and carefully developed drama structures will extend educators' and children's understandings alike. *More Stories! More Drama!* provides new and rich resources for teachers and students. It deserves to be in every teacher's hands.

Robyn Ewing
University of Sydney
Australia

Acknowledgements

We are extremely grateful to the teachers and students of Victoria, Saanich and Sooke School Districts who invited us into their classrooms and helped us to pilot much of the material that appears in this book. We are also deeply grateful to our own pre-service teachers at the University of Victoria and our neighbours at the University of British Columbia, and to their instructors; their energy, enthusiasm and most importantly, their feedback has nourished our own practice and benefited these drama structures. Further afield, we are indebted to the responses and thoughtful reflections of teachers in Utah and Tennessee and members of the American Alliance for Theatre and Education who have worked with such commitment and shared so honestly; to the Sydney Theatre Company for its support of our work with their innovative professional development programme; to our colleagues at the University of Sydney, University of Auckland and University of Canterbury for their invitations to work with their students, and to drama teachers in Christchurch and Dunedin. We regret that an act of nature prevented us from working with the teachers and students of Selwyn House School in Christchurch but wish to note that their concern for our safety and the hospitality they extended will never be forgotten.

The story drama structure for *Rose Blanche* draws upon the work of Vivian Wall in *Drama: One Forum Many Voices, 1*(2), Spring 1993, and later became a teaching video and teacher's guide under the auspices of the Victoria Holocaust Remembrance and Education Society, Multiculturalism BC, and the Multicultural Programs of Canadian Heritage. We thank Dr Alison Preece for introducing us to *Tricycle*, Dr Monica Prendergast for seeing what we missed and Dr Peter O'Connor and Briar O'Connor for their perceptive comments. Dr Jonothan Neelands introduced us to *The Composition* and to some of the strategies we use, as well as providing the stimulus for *Mary Ellery*. Dr Linda Laidlaw made early and wise contributions to *Wilfrid Gordon McDonald Partridge*. Leslie Hogya put us onto *The Follower* after she had used it with her grade one students. Phil Duchene has taught almost every structure with his pre-service teachers as well as with his school students; he and Glenys Berry provided us with wonderful commentary on how the lessons unfold. There are so many colleagues and master teachers to whom we are indebted for their exemplary practice that reflects the theory in action. We have had rich conversations that have opened our eyes and expanded our thinking.

Our first volume of story drama structures was nurtured by Lisa Barnett of Heinemann who encouraged many of us to write about our practice. Her advice and concern was invaluable to our field; her loss was grievous. We wish to acknowledge the care and interest of Intellect and its amazing staff of editors and marketing personnel, especially the tactful concern and teacherly eye of Richard Kerr. Their ability to recognize the need to expand the theatre and drama lists to include educational drama texts means that our field can continue to grow. It is a pleasure to be involved with such forward-thinking individuals.

And finally we thank Dr Robyn Ewing for her great support, her encouragement, and for inviting us to learn alongside her and her students. She introduced us to her favourite bookstores and to the work of Gary Crew and Steven Woolman—creators of two stories that have kept us awake many nights. Her recommendations always included a number of winners that we happily carried back to Canada to provide us with sustenance and pleasure. Robyn is a brilliant advocate for the arts, for drama and for literacy. It is her voice that we tend to hear most as we are writing; we are so pleased that she has agreed to be a part of this volume.

Victoria, British Columbia 2015

Chapter One

Towards a Humanizing Curriculum

> Drama can be thought of as a metaphor for bending time and space to create a space for exploratory interaction, dialogues, and representations out of which new thoughts, ideas and ways of looking/seeing can emerge.
>
> (Robyn Ewing, 2010, p. 40)

This new text, like *Into the Story: Language in Action through Drama* (2004), comprises a series of story drama structures that use picture books as their contexts for exploration. Picture books build connections to learning experiences for students, and when coupled with drama strategies promote a literacy that is three-dimensional, engaging students through mind, body and feeling. Story drama structures provide the integrating process frequently lacking in a fragmented and often overloaded curriculum; they go beyond the short term and present a cohesive approach to learning. It is the specificity of the drama strategies that makes these lessons unique and encourages teachers to embrace drama pedagogy as holistic education in its richest sense.

Since the publication of *Into the Story*, story drama structures have had wide recognition both nationally and internationally. This book brings together a second collection that uncovers curriculum in ways that are new for students and teachers both experienced and inexperienced in drama. It not only addresses such subjects as language arts, social studies and environmental education, it also explores areas of the "hidden" curriculum; for example, inter and intra personal communication, ethics and social justice. Each structure has been piloted with pre-service teachers and with teachers and students in elementary, middle school and secondary classrooms. We do not provide a synopsis of each story as there are many children's literature websites that provide a diversity of synopses and reviews of the stories included here. We do, however, provide the rationale for our choice of each book that should enable teachers to make their own decisions based on the content, themes and learning described. As in our first text, these stories have been organized with the developmental level of the students in mind. However, we have deliberately chosen not to be grade specific. While you might not consider *The Follower* as appropriate for middle or upper level students, it can be a wonderful source for advanced students who are working in media studies. The structures are open to adaptation. We know of middle-school students working with *Woolvs in the Sitee* while *Wilfrid Gordon McDonald Partridge* is a wonderful resource for senior citizens and as a part of local community activities. These stories seem to be effective with people of all ages, addressing the many forms of social languages that may be represented both inside classrooms and beyond.

> "Those Shoes" was hands-down the best drama workshop I have run thus far. Consumerism and materialism are issues I feel strongly about, and I found the structure really made it a relevant issue to my students. I took your plan and broke it into two lessons with some minor tweaks. Both lessons ran almost 90 minutes, but it felt like 15. There is so much variety that the kids were constantly engaged, and the final discussion was so great. Almost everyone shared a story about being excluded, or feeling ashamed about not having name-brand clothes. I also lent my plans to a colleague across the hall, and he had equally positive things to say about it.
>
> Shaun Sarton,
> pre-service teacher, 2015

Why Do We Need Another Book?

The continuing responses to *Into the Story* tell us that many teachers are looking for innovative methods for teaching critical thinking, literacy and curriculum integration and that these structures provide a way of working that fulfils mandated curriculum, stimulates learning and generates interest and engagement in their students. Because the structures, while clear, are not confining, teachers themselves are comfortable using them.

The matrix enables both experienced and novice teachers and facilitators to adapt or to create new structures using stories that their students enjoy and are applicable to their own classroom contexts. For some, they apply the drama strategies independently in order to open up areas of curriculum where a human dimension may be critical to understanding.

As well, the nature of picture books is changing; many of the most effective are looking at the issues that face us in today's world. As curricula change and our understanding of how we learn expands, we see the value of drama as an imperative pedagogy for engaging learners. These new stories have a wide appeal that, by putting students at the centre of the text, ask them to see possible worlds from a multiplicity of perspectives, to encounter ideas and dilemmas that demand empathic attention, and to grapple with things that matter. Story dramas that are built around current concerns allow participants, in Maxine Greene's (1995) words, "to name what we see around us—the hunger, the passivity, the homelessness, the 'silences'. . . . [I]t requires imagination" she writes," "to be conscious of them, to find our own lived worlds lacking because of them" (p. 111). Many of the stories we have included are a means of generating rich conversations about abstract concepts that are often only situated in textbooks.

We are all aware that the isolating nature of technology, concerns about safety, privacy and the breakdown of social and cultural traditions, is changing relationships with and within our worlds. Classrooms have now become one of the few places where people can gather together to discover and practice the skills of social literacy, a term that for us encompasses many of the ideas that lie at the heart of the hidden curriculum—the unspoken rules of social encounter that are defined and reinforced within school contexts. It is there that students working together "hitchhike on each other's ideas and modify and extend [their] own meaning making" (Booth, 2014, np). The dynamic make-up of our classrooms, students' diversity and cultural contributions provide a rich context that challenge each participant to negotiate ways of becoming members of a classroom community that stands as a microcosm of the larger world. "If we begin to see things differently in our drama and theatre work," Jonothan Neelands (2006) tells us, "if we behave differently, if we see how we can 'act' upon the imagined worlds of our drama, then perhaps we also begin to see how the 'real' world can be 'acted on' and changed" (p. 55). Drama enables us to interrogate our learning, own it and make connections among, between and beyond ourselves.

The issues and events of this new century and its first decades have brought an increased attention to what is going on in schools. Although much of that interest is described as the need to maintain our competitive edge in learning, in reality it is driven by anxiety over the economic fragility many so-called "first world" nations are now facing, along with the serious questions of responsibility to others in the world who face greater challenges. Educators have become more aware of the centrality of imagination, collaboration and creativity as integral to growing a more effective and healthy sense of nationhood. "Creativity is a step beyond imagination because it requires that you actually do something rather than lie around thinking about it" (Robinson, 2009, p. 71). In a time when creativity, innovation and much of our economic health is dependent upon our abilities to communicate, and schools are increasingly seen as the laboratories for democratic life, "the quantity and quality of talk in the classroom . . . is an important part of preparing citizens to find and use their voices" (Bloem, Klooster, & Preece, 2008, p. 6). In drama, as John O'Toole (2015) points out, we both talk and walk: "we can *play* with reality to create alternative *fictional* realities that we can try out through the *pretence* . . . [to] ask previously unthought-of questions" (p. 119).

How Does Drama Work?

Drama reconfigures space and, in doing so, shifts the relationships of power and knowing. A visit to any school shows us that most of our classrooms are still organized within a proscenium relationship that has been around in theatre for at least the past three centuries. This mode of learning, characteristic of 90% of primary/elementary classroom instructional time in schools in North America, disconnects us from ourselves and those around us (Pianta, Belsky, Houts, & Morrison, 2007). Drama education is teaching "in the round", and because it is a collective process, it is often hard to spot the teacher. The circle is fluid with participants and teacher moving in and out as they respond to the situations.

Context

Because a story drama structure is always situated within a context that demands all kinds of talk, it offers possibilities for understanding content in ways that are constructive and collaborative because learning is embodied, enacted and social. Think of a context as a container that holds the meaning. It includes not only the story line (plot) but also the situations, thoughts, feelings and points of view of the people in that story who are engaged in working their way through the conditions in which they find themselves. Context "demands that we think it from the inside rather than to think over and about it" (Johnson & O'Neill, 1984, p. 142), so drama activities are always placed inside some kind of human dilemma. Working in context demands a different way of thinking and planning because most importantly, context is the site for the *collective* building of dramatic action and the making of meaning. Rather than each activity being linearly accessed (as in a plot), context enables participants, through manipulating time, place and roles, to explore the implications of situations *they* think significant.

Underlying everything Dorothy Heathcote has given us was her concern for things substantive. "Do children do things that matter?" she once asked, "and in doing those things, do they know that they matter too?" (O'Connor, 2012, p. 22). A context is worth investigating when it is rich with possibilities. For example, the pretext offered in *Mary Ellery* (Morgan & Saxton, 2006) is a very, very short story about space travel. Those few lines become a drama as students collectively discover and build the questions that lead them to imagine the story within the story that effects the lives of all those who dared to venture. Only by placing themselves in the future can they explore the past and that requires participants to bring their own personal contexts and feelings into play.

Drama educates through embodied learning in a multiplicity of metalanguages—what the joint declaration of the UNESCO World Arts Conference (2007) calls "the humanizing languages of the arts" (p. 2). A "humanizing curriculum [is one] in which more attention is given to developing compassion, empathy, tolerance, highly developed interpersonal skills and respect for difference" (Neelands, 2010, p. 125). It teaches students "many of the skills that they need to be everyday participants in our diverse and complex literate society" (O'Mara, 2008, p. 159) by exploring human behaviours and experiences in social circumstances under fictional pressure. This exploration becomes the material with which the metaphorical worlds are woven.

Fiction and the metaphoric world

Metaphor is a foundational construct of our art form; in theatre and drama we are always working in the "as if" fictional world of the narrative. In whatever artistic genre we are engaged, the artist, Jerome Bruner (1986) reminds us, "creates possible worlds through the metaphoric transformation of the ordinary" (p. 49). Metaphors, perhaps because they are experienced physically and through the senses, offer new and different ways to experience life—at once clearly understood and, at the same time, ambiguous.

Because almost all stories are concerned with relationships between people, understanding stories "entails an understanding of people and how their goals, beliefs and emotions interact with their behaviours" (Mar, Oatley, Hirsh, dela Paz, & Peterson, 2006, p. 696). It should not surprise us that as we engage with the metaphoric world, we may see changes in perspectives and attitudes because real-world processing and how we process stories are closely related (p. 697). Djikic, Oatley, Zoeterman, and Peterson (2009) write that it is the "quality of art-induced emotions—their complexity, depth, range, and intensity—that potentially facilitate the process of . . . change" (p. 28). Through the embodied metaphoric acts of the imagination in drama and theatre we create internal models that result in increased social and empathic awareness.

> I taught *Rose Blanche* to my Children's Theatre class and Theatre One. Both classes loved it. It was the very first time any of them had any Holocaust education—these are international kids: Americans, Saudis, Egyptians, Pakistanis, Malaysians, Koreans, Canadians—a huge mix. This was a pivotal moment for them all—I have never seen them so moved. Sometimes I was afraid to speak—I just let them speak.
>
> Charlotte Harvey,
> experienced international teacher, 2014

Conditional language

Another interesting realization is the relationship of language to the fictional "as if" world we explore through drama. Creative imagining can be encouraged by the use of conditional language (*"might", "may", "perhaps", "possibly"*) not only in our instructions but also in prompting participants' thinking and reflecting (Chanowitz & Langer, 1981). The research of Ellen Langer and her colleagues (1987, 1989) into the relationship between what they refer to as "conditional learning" and mindfulness has made us more aware of the significance of that kind of instructional language in drama. The use of the conditional creates a sense of uncertainty that helps us to become more aware of new things (Siegel, 2007). The conditional helps students to recognize that the nature of the world in both fiction and reality is always to be fluid. Much of the language we offer in these story drama structures is designed specifically to keep learners in the active role of mental processing as they make sense of content and its context. For example (from *"I longs for bloo skys"*), using the strategy of "spectrum of difference":

> In role as a member of this community, think about a word or phrase that most clearly reflects where you, yourself, stand in response to Ben's call. You may use your own words or something that you've read that speaks more directly to what you are thinking and feeling. As you make this choice, you need to think very carefully about what is happening in the city around you.
>
> Where do the dangers lie? What may be the consequences of joining Ben? How might your choice affect your family? Your own career? And the safety of those you love?

As Richard Sennett (2012) points out, this is the kind of language that is used by diplomats because it "open[s] up a space for experiment; tentativeness issue[s] an invitation to others to join in" (p. 22).

The Empathic Process

Part of mental processing involves the potential for students developing and refining their empathic responses. For many years, drama educators have been claiming that "walking in another's shoes" is a powerful means of developing empathy. Our research has shown that that is not necessarily so. Drama requires that we take on the role of another, imagining what it must be like to be someone else by "being able to infer the full range of mental states (beliefs, desires, intentions, imagination, emotions, etc.) that cause action" (Baron Cohen, 2001, p. 3). This ability is what is known as Theory of Mind but is only one part of an *empathic process*. Goldstein, Wu, and Winner (2009) example the bully who understands what a person is thinking and feeling but is not affected by it; the bully knows what buttons to press and understands the effect of his or her behaviour but doesn't care; Theory of Mind is a cognitive process of engagement. On the other hand, what we generally think of as "empathy" is another component of the process and is the result of directly experiencing another person's emotional state. Martin Buber (1965) describes this emotional engagement best as "glid[ing] with one's own feeling into the dynamic structure of [another] . . . to trace it from within . . . with the perceptions of one's own muscles" (p. 97). This is a deeper feeling of connection, a whole body response that attunes to others.

We wonder where else in a student's day, does he or she have the opportunity to explore the big questions but also to play inside them? It is not enough to do "improv", theatre sports, games and exercises; it is our responsibility as teachers to go beyond and deeper, providing "a sense of safe intimacy with a world we not only imagine, but also literally embody" (Wojciehowski & Gallese, 2011, p. 16). Through the playing we are developing and practicing the capacity for compassion: the generation of a need for action.

Compassion, according to Daniel Goleman (2006), is the final feature of the empathic process. Thinking and feeling as another is not enough; empathy requires that we respond with some kind of action; "I notice you, I feel with you, and so I act to help you" (p. 56). To stand with another—even in fictional circumstances—is to *practice* compassion. Nothing happens in drama without students taking action; making decisions as they take on roles, and carrying through with the choices they make (Neelands, 2010). There are many opportunities in these story drama structures to embody that practice, for as Paul Woodruff (2008) points out, in theatre and drama, "caring . . . may be make-believe for us, but it is real enough to count as practice for caring in real life" (p. 153). He later adds, "without action, what would be the use of caring?" (p. 158). This, surely, is the humanizing curriculum in action.

So let's get started with some suggestions for our practice.

How the Story Drama Structures Work

The following description comes directly from *Into the Story: Language in Action through Drama* (2004, pp. 6–8). We include it as there may be readers who are unfamiliar with the structures. Each structure is laid out in the same way.

- **Why Did We Choose This Story?** We begin by offering a rationale for the choice of the story. Within the rationale we describe themes, applications and suitability.
- **Key Understandings and Questions** lie at the heart of the story and provide the direction of the drama and the reference points for reflection. Drama works best when the affective and the effective are integrated as universal understandings or questions; these may differ, depending on a person's experience, interests and culture.

The organization of each activity is consistent throughout. We give each activity a number and a title and suggest approximate times.

- **Grouping** refers to the class configuration (e.g., pairs, whole class).
- **Strategy** names the activity; the description of the strategy is embedded in the teacher talk/instruction. We have included a concise explanation of each strategy in the Glossary for further reference.
- **Administration** includes the space requirements as well as specific materials required for the activity.
- **Focus** provides the *why* or objective of the activity and answers that question, "Why are we doing this?", or "Why are you doing this with your students?"
- **Options** are activities that we offer either as an adaptation or alternative activity for, say, younger students or as a means of extending literacy skills using the drama as a meaningful context.
- **Extensions** are based upon specific activities that teachers have used to extend the drama experience or to integrate it into other curriculum areas.
- **Resources** provide references for either the teacher or the students.
- A summary list of **Materials** according to strategy acts as a quick and useful reminder.
- **Reflection** is an important part of effective drama. It occurs *throughout* the structures, sometimes as a way to think about where we have been in order to know where we are and/or where we need to go. Reflection also serves as a way of processing what has happened and, especially in the final activities, to help us move beyond the particulars of the story to the more universal implications.
- **Questions** are another important component of drama and are used extensively throughout. The questions that stimulate the most effective thought are open,

allowing students to contribute their own ideas and appreciate the perspectives and ideas of others.

The structures serve teachers as complete frameworks of organization for understanding how strategies and techniques can be used to deepen the drama. They offer examples of how one activity is linked to another. Linking is a critical means of achieving coherence in the flow of meaning, not only for the students, but also for the teacher. Linking activities to create a dramatic flow that moves the story forward while at the same time deepening meaning is fundamental to effective drama and is rarely addressed in the literature of practice. Linking is one of the most important elements in planning in drama.

The detailed instructions for the individual activities can provide templates for use in other situations. As teachers and students become more comfortable using the structures, they will soon see how to apply drama strategies to other contexts.

Ideas for Classroom Implementation

Timing

These story drama structures may take from one-and-half hours to three hours. They need time to unfold, but with specific activities, it may work best if you give students less time, helping them to focus, to learn to work efficiently and effectively and expanding as needed. It may be helpful to ask them how much time they think they need. We have found that the more experienced the group, the more time they may require.

You will notice that throughout the structures and within the context of the instructions, we use phrases such as [They do], [They write], [They share], etc. These indicate that time should be provided for thinking, doing, sharing—all necessary components of teaching.

You may find that you only do a few of the activities in any given lesson, in which case the structure can extend over a number of days. On the other hand, you may choose to select only a few of the activities. It all depends on your focus, your time and your students' interests and needs. You can also use any of the strategies as part of lessons in other subject areas.

Instruction

While the language of the structure appears to be very specific for the teacher, it is intended to offer an open structure for the students, inviting them to become co-creators. For that reason we rarely include student responses. Student comments are only exampled when they may help the teacher to be aware of the kinds of things students might say (Miller & Saxton, 2004, p. 6).

All of these structures are written in teacher action language. We always carry the structure with us as we teach; it keeps us on track as there are many times when the discussion can take different directions. The sequencing, the questions, the transitions are all ways to move the drama into a deeper place but what is happening between you and your students will provide further guidance. For those of you who would like to know more about the drama strategies and techniques used, we provide a Glossary of Terms as well as a list of Recommended Reading.

Teacher in role

There are times in the structures when the teacher is in role. It is a powerful strategy and one that engages all students. Using teacher in role changes the classroom dynamic as it shifts the status and power by allowing you to play inside the story with your students. For example, when you take on the role of someone who does not know, needs help, or has been away and wants to know what has happened, the students become the ones who hold the knowledge.

Being in role is not about acting but rather about taking on the perspectives and attitudes of another. There is no rule about "once in role you have to stay there". You can go in and out of role as long as you tell them; young children do this regularly when they are playing. It is sometimes really useful to stop for a moment and come out of role to take stock of what's happening. However, there is one guiding rule for being in role: take the work seriously. If it matters to you, it will matter to your students.

Reflection

Every drama structure offers opportunities for reflection. Key understandings and questions lie at the heart of the story and provide the direction of the drama and the reference points for reflection. These are not usually shared with the students directly but are embedded in the kinds of reflection suggested both inside and outside the drama. Spectrum of difference (cited above) is an example of reflection inside the drama. Questions throughout (whether inside or outside the drama) provide the prompts for students to consider the implications of their work. The reflection after the conclusion of the drama is designed to draw out the key understandings and questions that act as the wider curricula subtext.

> I have spent the week with *Woolvs in the Sitee* ... At the moment I am teaching my primary (elementary) teacher education students in their introduction to teaching the arts curriculum unit. I made a deliberate choice to work from practical experience to theoretical concepts and seized upon your story drama structure to model practice. In all I have worked with it three times, each time different but the same structure .... *Woolvs* is such a beautiful pre-text with so many open-ended possibilities ....
>
> Robin Pascoe
> Senior lecturer, Arts & Drama Education, 2009

Multiple perspectives

Central to critical pedagogy is the ability to see the world from many points of view. These drama structures ask students to work from different outlooks; their lenses shift as they move back and forth, challenging stereotypes, exploring alternatives and questioning motives. As you may be aware, this is not generally the way it is in classrooms and therefore students may be concerned that their thinking and feeling may not match accepted classroom thought. That is why the building of community and a safe environment are important components of the drama classroom and makes it possible for students to engage in what for them may be risk-taking.

Assessment

Assessment is often a stumbling block because of the nature of learning. We are working with content in which there may be no right answers. In these drama structures there are no tests and no essays. That is not to say that the work is not rigorous and rich—two of the components of the complexity curriculum. Something like writing in role places many demands on students, including the ability to take perspectives that may be contrary to their beliefs; tableaux is about being able to be still and silent—easy enough to assess—but that's about mechanics and not about what is really important, which is making meaning. When the whole class is working in pairs improvising, how is it possible to assess each individual student at the same time? And would it be fair to do so because improvising is about working interactively and interdependently?

Of course, we are capable of assessing but what we are looking for in drama is different. Let's begin by remembering that whatever the content, a teacher knows a good lesson by the tone, energy and quality of student engagement. In drama:

- We are able to see and hear that engagement when ideas are being worked out physically and/or verbally through talk, discussion, argument and negotiation.
- As you move around the room, students are able to articulate what they are doing and why they are doing it.
- The talk should reflect the vocabulary of the discipline, and a presentation (of whatever kind) should reflect the development of discipline skills (i.e. are they working safely? With focus?)
- Students are able to talk to each other and with you about how the task they are engaged in relates to what they have done and how it can further the drama.
- The purpose of the work is to deepen the drama, not to provide entertainment for peers. It is not difficult to hear the difference between laughter generated genuinely as part of the work and laughter geared to playing up to the audience or at the expense of others. Drama is about thinking and hard work. Students often refer to this as "fun" and you will know the difference between this kind of fun and "fooling around".
- In response to questions that are open and invitational, students demonstrate that they too can generate new questions and thoughtful reflections. Their contributions deepen understanding, not just of the issues within the drama structure, but how those issues may connect to their own lives.

Drama is a social art form that must operate collectively and collaboratively. This highly demanding discipline requires the development of skills that will be reflected in the energy and commitment of students. You can see this in the doing and in the quality of that doing described above. As students mature they may create their own criteria and self- and peer assessments. Of course, you know your own class and will have curriculum documents to guide the criteria you may want to apply. There are a number of texts listed in Recommended Reading that address how we gather information and value learning in drama.

Making a Story Drama Structure

Picture books are rich resources of learning for all ages and you, your own students and librarians will have many suggestions. The strategies are generic and may be used across the curriculum whenever you sense that learning might be expanded and/or deepened through drama. In the Appendix, we offer some suggestions that you may find useful should you wish to design your own story drama structures.

Effective drama allows everyone to develop their interpersonal skills through collaborative, cooperative dialogues that generate a multiplicity of perspectives and responses. In other words, it is not "just the facts and skills we teach, but the knowledge we create together and the understandings and connections that each learner makes from that knowledge" (Wolk, 2008, p. 118). It is through practice in these embodied conversations that respect for difference may be internalized. We hope the stories in this collection offer opportunities to engage with fictional situations that generate new ways of thinking about the world.

Chapter Two

And Quick as That

Based on *The Follower,* written by Richard Thompson and illustrated by Martin Springett

Why Did We Choose This Story?

Although naturally appropriate for younger students, this is a story that everyone enjoys exploring. Like all good stories it has a mystery at its heart that generates concerns and queries that linger long after the experience. As well,

- It is particularly appropriate for fall and winter seasons because the text captures the sense of weather.
- Like *The House that Jack Built*, in this cumulative story the language is strongly patterned and full of imagery, as are the illustrations. Both may give rise to equally rich movement.
- Central to the story and to each illustration are the questions, Who is the woman, where does she go, why does she go there, and who follows her?

Key Understandings and Questions

- Being needed is fundamental to a well-balanced existence.
- What is it that an animal companion can offer that is special?
- How does the tension between the elements of theatre (sound/silence, movement/stillness, light/dark) enhance our understanding of the text?

1. Preparing to enter the story — ***5 minutes***

Grouping:	**Whole class in a circle**
Strategy:	**Movement**
Administration:	**Tambourine**
Focus:	**Exploring space and pace**

Teacher: Before we begin our drama, we are going to warm up our bodies, as well as our imaginations. You will have to concentrate really hard to remember who you are. As I go around the circle, I will give each of you a letter: A, B or C. Listen carefully so that you can remember.

As raise your hands, Bs raise your hands, Cs raise your hands.

It is useful to check with the students before beginning the activity.

Teacher: When I give the signal, As, you are to move *quickly* around the room, Bs move at a *normal* pace, Cs move *very slowly*. Be very careful not to bump into anyone. Keep good spaces between each other.

When you hear the tambourine, stop. Listen to the next instruction.

Ready? Off you go.

After a few moments, sound the tambourine.

Change. This time Bs move *very slowly,* Cs move *quickly* and As move at a *normal* pace.

As above.

Teacher: Now, the last time: Cs move at a *normal* pace, Bs move *quickly* and As move *very slowly.*

And freeze. Please sit down where you are.

Choose one of those speeds and think about what it brought to into your mind; what situations were you reminded of? Talk with the people next to you. [They talk]

Who heard something they would like to share with the group? [*Hear*]

2. Into the story ***10 minutes***

Grouping:	**Whole class**
Strategy:	**Reading a picture**
Administration:	**Overhead projector (OHP) or other media; illustration of Thursday's storm.**
Focus:	**To mine the illustration for the details of the story**

Teacher: Now, let's move into our story. Make sure you can see the screen clearly. [They shift]

Look at this picture. [*Up on OHP or other media*]

What do you see? Where do you see that?

It is important for the students to be able to justify their observations.

Teacher: What do you hear? Where do you see that?

How does the movement we have just done connect to this picture? [*Hear*]

How many of you have been in weather like this? [They raise hands] Tell your partner about that experience. [They do]

Has anyone anything they would like to share?

3. Sounds of the storm ***7 minutes***

Grouping:	**Whole group as above**
Strategy:	**Soundscape**
Administration:	**Picture as above; chalk board and chalk or chart paper and pen**
Focus:	**To give a sense of reality to the wind**

Teacher: Let's see if we can make the picture come alive through sound.

What sorts of sounds might we hear? Look carefully at the picture again, what possibilities for sound lie in this picture?

As students offer, words are recorded.

Teacher: Let's try to turn these words into their sounds. Let's start at the top of our list. Anyone who feels that they can make that word or those words come alive as sound, on the count of three, just go for it! [They do]

I wonder how we could orchestrate those sounds to make the story of the weathery day? In drama, we call this a *Soundscape.*

What sounds shall we begin with? What will we layer in and how will we end it? [They suggest]

List the order on the board for a guide.

Teacher: Let's try it and see how it sounds? [They try it]

Who has a suggestion to make our soundscape more weathery? [*Listen to suggestions*]

If there is time, students may like to do this more than once.

4. Bringing the picture alive ***7 minutes***

Grouping:	**Whole class as above; individual movement**
Strategy:	**Movement; tableau; creating titles**
Administration:	**Illustration as above; Music such as *Sinfonia Antartica* (Vaughn Williams' Symphony No. 7) *Landscape* (cut #3); tambourine**
Focus:	**To find ways of moving that create a sense of the illustration**

Teacher: Now, what about the movement that is here in this picture. Look carefully. Apart from the woman, what else is moving in the picture? [They identify]

These words may be listed on the board.

Teacher: Find your own space in the room. Close your eyes.

In a moment, we are going to make the picture come alive through movement, but first, let's hear some music that might help us with our movement as we create a certain mood—a certain feeling—that we see in the picture. [They hear 30 seconds to a minute]

Now, as you listen to the music, choose to be one of the things that were moving in the picture. [*Music on*]

Teacher speaks over the music.

Teacher: Let the music help your body find that shape and movement of the thing you have chosen. Experiment moving as that shape as you listen to the music. Keep your eyes closed while you do this. [They do for about a minute]

Relax for a moment.

We'll do it again, but this time when you hear the tambourine, you will freeze in whatever shape your body is in at that moment. [They work for 30 seconds to the music and freeze to the tambourine]

Without shifting your bodies and using only your peripheral vision, look around you. [They do]

As you look around, think about what we might title our frozen picture—our tableau? The words have to match what we see.

Good. Relax. Let's have your ideas. [They share titles]

5. Putting it all together ***5 minutes***

Grouping:	**Whole class divided into two groups**
Strategy:	**Soundscape and movement**
Administration:	**Music as above; tambourine for control if needed; dark cloak or raincoat with hood; walking stick**
Focus:	**To add a new element to what is already known; to improvise responses**

Teacher: Now, we are going to form two groups.

Teacher divides the class in half.

One group will re-create the soundscape and the other will re-create the movement.

Who would be willing to lead our orchestra—to be the conductor?

There may be more than one conductor because it can be done more than once.

Teacher: Where will our orchestra be? [They decide]

Before we begin, let's add to our picture. Is there someone who is prepared to take the role of the woman in the picture? She will be moving through our landscape.

If a number of students volunteer, choose one and suggest we can do this more than once.

Teacher: Where is the road that the woman will walk upon? [They decide]

Where will she begin and where will she stop? [They decide]

Decide where you need to be in order to create this moving picture? [They find their positions]

After the stage has been "set", offer the following,

Teacher: I wonder if this cloak (and stick) will help us to believe that this is the woman in our story? Let's try it.

Are we ready?

Let's begin with the soundscape to set the mood. And when those of you who are creating the environment feel it is right, begin your movement.

Woman, when the environment is established, begin your journey along the road.

Let's rehearse. Conductor, whenever you are ready. [They rehearse]

After the first time through,

Teacher: Just talk to the person next to you about that. [They do]

Has anyone any comments? [*Listen*]

If we were to do it again, what could we suggest that would help us to believe that it is real? [They suggest]

Based on students' responses, this scene can be replayed any number of times, using a different student in role as the woman and switching the orchestra and the environment groups; each experience will feed the new role(s).

Note: If the story drama structure is to take more than one lesson, this is a good place to break. For the new lesson, the game of "Grandmother's Footsteps" (dramaresource.com) will provide preparation for the improvised activity and serve as a way to refocus the students on the drama.

6. Introducing the story ***5 minutes***

Grouping:	**Whole class**
Strategy:	**Reading aloud**
Administration:	**Text of *The Follower***
Focus:	**To bring their pre-story experiences to the listening of the story**

Teacher: Find a place where you can see the pictures. [They do]

Teacher reads the whole story of The Follower, *sharing the illustrations.*

7. Using the story for improvisation ***10 minutes***

Grouping:	**Pairs**
Strategy:	**Shadowing**
Administration:	**Chart paper; pen; music (as in Activity #4)**
Focus:	**To recall events in the story; to explore improvising in movement and with words**

Teacher: Who can remember some of the things the woman did to try to get rid of the cat? [*Write up on chart paper*]

Find a partner and a place in the room where you can work together without disturbing others.

Choose who will be A and who will be B.

As, we are going to imagine that we are the woman.

Bs, we are going to imagine that we are the shadowy cats following the woman.

Set yourselves up as the woman and the cat, ready to begin with the music.

When you hear the tambourine; As, turn to see if something is following you. Let's recall some of the things the woman said or did to the cat? [They suggest]

Bs, your task is to stop *so still* that when the woman turns to see you, she won't see you moving, however quickly she turns.

As, you may want to add what the woman did or said as you turn.

Music on and freeze. You may do this five or six times.

Teacher: Talk to your partner about that. What made it real for you both?

Everyone, switch roles with your partner and do again. But when you hear the tambourine for the last time—and I will say, "Last time"—the woman will turn and invite the cat to come in.

Anyone remember the words she said? [They suggest]

Good. You may use those words but if you can't remember them, use whatever words seem right for you.

Ready? Begin. [They do]

Music on and freeze two or three times before saying,

<u>Teacher:</u> Last time. [They improvise]

Well done. How was it different this last time? [They share]

<u>8. Extending the story</u> ***<u>7 minutes</u>***

Grouping: **Whole class working individually**

Strategy: **Writing in role**

Administration: **Paper and pencils**

Focus: **To reflect inside the story**

<u>Teacher:</u> Find your own private place and listen carefully as I pass out paper and pencils to everyone.

Speaking as the materials are passed out,

<u>Teacher:</u> Imagine you are the woman. Your friend lives very far away and has no idea that you have adopted a cat.

Write to your friend, telling what it was that made you decide (after all that time rejecting it) that you would take this cat into your house. What is it about this cat that made you change your mind?

Begin writing and don't worry about spelling or punctuation, just explain your decision to your friend. [They write]

It is important not to rush through this strategy. Don't worry if students stop writing. You can say quietly, "I can see that some people are thinking very deeply about what they are writing." *When most students appear to have finished,*

<u>Teacher:</u> Stop now and re-read your letter.

Underline the sentence that best explains your reason for keeping the cat. Commit that reason to memory. [They do]

9. Discovering the reasons behind the ending of the story — 5 minutes

Grouping:	**Whole class working individually**
Strategy:	**Tapping in**
Administration:	**None**
Focus:	**To concretize thinking and feeling; to justify a decision**

Teacher: In a moment, we are going to hear those reasons. I will go around and put my hand on your shoulder. When you feel my hand on your shoulder, we will hear why you have decided to keep the cat.

In order to hear better, let's put on our cat's ears and listen for the reason that makes us feel most wanted.

Move around the room, placing your hand firmly on each student's shoulder. Leave your hand there until the student stops speaking. After each one has contributed,

Teacher: Thank you. There were some excellent reasons for keeping the cat. Just turn to the person next to you and talk about what you heard and which reason or reasons you think would make a cat feel wanted.

If you conclude here, you will want to reflect on the whole process. Notice how these questions begin to unpack the Key Understandings and Questions.

If you decide on using further strategies (see below), you will want to return to these questions to help you and your students reflect on the story and their work.

Teacher: I wonder why this cat chose this particular woman? Many people must have walked along that road, why this woman?

A lot of us have pets. I wonder what is it about a pet that makes us want to keep it?

In drama, we talk about going into the story. How did the work we did with "Thursday's picture" prepare us to enter the story?

Extensions

Teacher in role:

What sorts of questions would we like to ask the woman? [Teacher then goes into role (using the cloak?) and responds to their questions]

Or

Why would I want a cat? What's a cat good for?

Or

I've never had a cat before. I am hoping that you can tell me how to look after one.

Brainstorming:

What are suitable names for a cat? Which name(s) would be appropriate for this cat?

Writing an instructional pamphlet:

How to make your cat feel at home.

Message writing:

What was the message that caused the woman make the journey?

Imagining a life:

Where might the woman be going every evening?

What, or who, calls her out and why, I wonder?

I wonder who might be at home to look after her child?

Thinking from the cat's point of view:

What might the cat do to help the woman?

Exploring your inner cat:

We are really pleased to be able to include the following extension that comes from our colleague, Phil Duchene, who describes how he and his grade one/two students concluded the story drama structure:

> After the cat had safely "sidled in" and we'd thought about what cats might need, I closed the lesson by reading and paraphrasing The Naming of Cats,

the poem at the very end of *Old Possum's Book of Practical Cats* (Eliot, 1968) to the effect that cats really had three names. You know how it goes: there is the "sensible" name, the one "that the family use daily"; a second "particular, dignified" name; with the third being the cat's name that belongs to no-one but him/her self and about which the cat often "meditates". And we talked about what cats are really thinking about in their apparent meditations—who they are and what they like—and I think the kids got the metaphor. We created these contemplative cats in suitable poses in their new homes with the witch character. It was a way of exploring that wobbly Platonic idea of "catness", perhaps. We did some sculpting of cats in contemplation. Good tactile stuff. We ended with the Jellicle Chorus; its relentless rhythm gets a life and starts milling movements of its own … Best, Phil

PS. We didn't even get to Andrew Lloyd Webber! (Email, February 5, 2015).

Materials

Activity 1: Tambourine
Activity 2: OHP or other media and illustration of Thursday's storm
Activity 3: Illustration as above; chalk board, chalk or chart paper, pens
Activity 4: Illustration as above; music: Symphony No. 7: *Sinfonia Antartica*, cut no. 3 (*Landscape*) or other similar music; tambourine
Activity 5: Music as above; tambourine; cloak or dark raincoat with hood; walking stick
Activity 6: Text of *The Follower*
Activity 7: Chart paper, pen; music as above
Activity 8: Paper and pencils
Activity 9: Students' written work

Resource

Thompson, R. (2000). *The follower*. Toronto, ON: Fitzhenry & Whiteside.

Chapter Three

Memories for Miss Nancy

Based on *Wilfrid Gordon McDonald Partridge,* written by Mem Fox and illustrated by Julie Vivas

Why Did We Choose This Story?

- It is a story with wide appeal for all ages.
- It offers us a way to celebrate the contributions that elders make to our lives.
- The text and illustrations appeal both to children and adults.
- Most children have a means of finding a personal connection. All of them have grandparents and, often, great grandparents. Not all children are able to know these family elders. Nevertheless, there is, for most children, a sense of their family's history and their place in it.
- Working with this story opens up the possibilities for making connections with Seniors in retirement homes.

Key Understandings and Questions

- What importance do memories play in our lives?
- What is it about intergenerational relationships that hold special meaning?
- Anyone at any age is capable of compassionate action.

1. Setting the context ***5 minutes***

Grouping:	**Whole group**
Strategy:	**Discussion**
Administration:	**None**
Focus:	**How are we different from when we were little?**

Teacher: What do you remember about when you were little?

I wonder how you are different from when you were in preschool? Kindergarten? Grade one?

What sorts of changes have happened to you as you have grown?

Here the discussion is open and invitational. All children can contribute.

Teacher: Today's drama has a lot to do with change and remembering, so you'll want to remember some of the things we have just heard.

2. Looking for change ***5 minutes***

Grouping:	**Pairs**
Strategy:	**Exercise**
Administration:	**None**
Focus:	**Observation**

Teacher: We are going to do an exercise to help us get ready for our drama today.

You will need to find a partner. [*There may be a group of three; that's not a problem*]

Stand up and face one another. [They do]

Look very carefully at each other. [They do]

What do you notice? Don't tell, just look. [They do]

Now, each of you turn back to back. [They do]

Your task is to change one thing about your appearance. When you have each changed one thing, tell your partner that you are ready.

When you are both ready, turn around and face each other. [They do]

Can you see what has been changed? Tell your partner the change you see. [They do]

Well done!

You may want to model this activity by turning your back to the students and changing something, asking them if they are ready to observe closely. Turn around and let them guess. You can make this pretty obvious in order to ensure success. Note: Be sure that you are wearing something that you can easily change!

3. The oldest person ***10 minutes***

Grouping: **Same pairs as above**

Strategy: **Storytelling**

Administration: **Stickies; a large sheet of chart paper on the floor**

Focus: **Remembering**

Teacher: Today's drama has a lot to do with change and remembering.

We all know someone who is much older than we are and who might have a memory of what we were like when we were little.

I am going to tell you about the oldest person I know and a memory I have of her/him. [*Teacher does*]

Who is the oldest person you have known? That person may be dead or may be alive. Tell your partner and then write the name and age on a piece of sticky paper. [They do]

Let's gather in a circle to hear these stories. [They do]

Who would like to tell us something about their person? When you have finished, please come and put your sticky on this paper on the floor.

When all the stories have been shared, hang up the paper on the board.

Teacher: So even though we change and grow, we still keep those memories inside us.

Note: If you want to take less time or if the children have difficulty with writing, you can write the names and ages and put them up as each child remembers a story.

OPTION

4. Special memories ***30–40 minute lesson***

Grouping: **New partners**

Strategy: **Storytelling**

Administration: **3–4 paper bags; 3 x 5 note cards**

Focus: **Finding connections to the stories of others**

Teacher: Think back to a special memory that you shared with an older person. Tell your partner about that time. [They do]

Think back on the story you just told. What is one word that you could use to describe that time? Write the one word on a note card and when you have finished come up and put your card in one of these paper bags. [They do]

Thank you, there must be some wonderful words hidden in these bags!

Now, I'm going to pass the bags around.

As teacher is talking, s/he begins to move around the group.

Teacher: Each of you is to put your hand into one of the bags and choose a new card. Read what is written on it.

What new memory from your own life is triggered by that word that you just chose? What memory does that word remind you of? Tell your partner. [They do]

Who would like to share their memory with all of us? Before you begin, be sure to tell us the word that you are using, so that the author of the word can recognize it.

After the student has shared his/her memory,

Would the person of that original word like to tell us about his/her memory?

This lesson can be the basis of a writing project that brings together student stories from their memories, accompanied by illustrations. Students can also ask their parents about a special memory that they have of their own childhood or of the student when he or she was little.

5. The story ***5 minutes***

Grouping: **Whole class**
Strategy: **Story reading**
Administration: **Text of *Wilfrid Gordon McDonald Partridge***
Focus: **Listening and engagement with the problem**

Teacher: I think we are ready to begin our story now.

Teacher reads the story from the beginning to:

***So Wilfrid Gordon went home again to look for* something that would help Miss Nancy remember.**

[*Teacher closes the book*]

Note adapted text above.

6. Going into role ***5 minutes***

Grouping:	**Groups of four**
Strategy:	**Thinking in role**
Administration:	**Old photo album**
Focus:	**Entering the story**

Teacher: Groups of four, please.

I'd like each of you to put yourself into Wilfrid Gordon's shoes. You will have to use your imaginations to do that.

Talk in your groups about what it is that you think you could give or show to Miss Nancy that would help her to remember again.

Allow about five minutes for students to discuss their ideas. As the students discuss, the teacher moves around from group to group, listening and noting ideas. When time is up,

Teacher: I heard some wonderful ideas

Teacher reflects back some of the ideas that she heard in the groups and then says,

I overheard someone mention photographs. I wonder if we could create the photographs that might have been pasted into this old photo album [*Teacher holds up the album*] so long ago? Are you ready to try that?

7. Exploring Miss Nancy's life *7 minutes*

Grouping: **Same groups of four**

Strategy: **Tableau; captioning**

Administration: **Caption strips; an old photo album; old photos that give a sense of family/friends in the 20s, 30s or 40s; one photo must have an easily readable caption under it; a shawl of a good length [*The Family of Man* (LIFE monograph) is an excellent resource]**

Focus: **To help students find connections**

Teacher: Let's think about the people in Miss Nancy's photo album. Who might they be? [They offer]

For example, let's look at this picture. [*Teacher holds up an old photo*]

Who might these people be? [They offer]

Where do you suppose this photo was taken? [They offer]

Now, look at this one.

Teacher shows another photo with a caption written under it,

What can you tell about this picture? The caption will help us.

Imagine what other pictures might be in this album.

Share your ideas with your group. [They do]

Now, you are going to be creating with your bodies a picture that would be in Miss Nancy's photo album.

This picture has a very special name in drama. It is called a *tableau.*

Some of the tableaux you make might be of when Miss Nancy was a little girl. Some might be of when she was a teenager or when she was your Mum's age, or some might be when she was a grandma.

Just before we begin, let's look at these photographs again. Do the people move? Do they speak? [They respond]

So, in our tableaux, we won't be able to move or speak either.

The tableau that you make will have Miss Nancy in it.

In your tableau, once you have decided how old Miss Nancy is and what your picture is about, choose someone to take on the responsibility of becoming Miss Nancy in the tableau.

Everybody in the group will be in the photograph with Miss Nancy, so you must show us a picture that will have everyone in your group in it. Off you go. [They begin to work]

After the teacher sees that they are forming their idea for their tableau, s/he suggests:

Teacher: Just stop your work for a moment. I can see that you're just about ready and there are some wonderful photographs of Miss Nancy's life. You now have two more decisions to make.

First: We need a caption for our photographs. What will your caption say about your picture? I will give each group a caption strip and a pen.

What will your caption, the writing under the photograph, tell us about your tableau? [Groups complete their captions]

Well done!

Now the second decision that you have to make is about using a prop to help us recognize Miss Nancy in your tableau. The prop for each Miss Nancy will be this shawl. [*Holds up shawl*]

This shawl can be transformed into whatever you need to help us to see Miss Nancy. For example, it could be used as an apron, Miss Nancy's blanket, a bag or basket of some sort. You must decide, in the next minute, how you will use the shawl. When your time comes to present your tableau, I will give you the shawl to use. Is everybody clear? [They decide]

Good!

8. Viewing the tableaux ***6–7 minutes***

Grouping: **As above. Groups are placed around the circle, so that every group can see each presentation without having to move**

Strategy: **Tableau; Tapping in (optional technique, see below)**

Administration: **The shawl**

Focus: **To appreciate each other's work; to see the skills of tableau-making in action; writing Miss Nancy's life**

Teacher: We're going to see these tableaux as if we were turning the pages of this old photograph album. When it's your turn, the rest of us will close our eyes as you get ready. I will give the group the shawl to indicate who is Miss Nancy. Don't forget to put your caption on the floor in front of your photograph.

When I count to 3, we'll open our eyes and see the photograph as it appears in Miss Nancy's album. We will be able to recognize Miss Nancy because she will be using the shawl. I will read the caption out loud to help us understand the picture. And then we will take another moment to look really hard. Those of you in the tableau will need to concentrate and focus. Remember that you can't move and you can't speak.

As each group finishes (without reflection), they sit down and the teacher moves to the next group in turn and gives the shawl to that group. She signals as above.

The teacher may choose to hear the thinking of some of the people in the picture:

OPTION

8a. Viewing the tableaux — ***6–7 minutes***

Grouping:	**As above. Groups are placed around the circle so that every group can see each presentation without having to move**
Strategy:	**Tapping in**
Administration:	**The shawl**
Focus:	**To express thoughts in role**

Teacher: I am going to stand just outside the picture with my hand on someone's shoulder.

I'm going to ask that person who is now in role: "What are you thinking as your picture is being taken?" [S/he responds]

Note: The teacher may ask students if there is someone else in the tableau they would like to hear from. Teacher does not need to tap into everyone in the picture. This technique is meant for clarification and to deepen students' engagement in the work.

9. Memories from time past ***5 minutes***

Grouping:	**Individual**
Strategy:	**Writing in role**
Administration:	**Paper and pencil**
Focus:	**Helping a friend to remember**

Teacher: Those were wonderful pictures and we know so much more about Miss Nancy's life now.

I wonder if you could write a letter to Miss Nancy reminding her of your special time together. Perhaps your letters will help her to remember.

Go and find your own space and imagine what you would say to Miss Nancy to remind her of that special time that you shared so long ago. I will come around and give you a piece of paper and a pencil.

As s/he is doing this, teacher says,

You might start your letter with: "Dear Miss Nancy, Do you remember …?"

Or

"Dear Miss Nancy, I was just remembering the time when …"

Or

"Dear Miss Nancy, I just came across your picture and was thinking back to the time when …"

Students begin writing. Allow them time to think. Often when they stop writing, they will go back to it as new ideas come to them and as they are encouraged by others still writing. Do not hurry this process.

Note: If the students are not capable of writing on their own, you may choose to do a group-write on the chalk board or on chart paper. In this case, let the children have time to think about their special memory and then solicit their ideas for a group letter.

10. Meeting Miss Nancy — ***3 minutes***

Grouping:	**Individual**
Strategy:	**Teacher in role; building an image**
Administration:	**Shawl; chair; old small wooden box big enough for letters beside the chair where students can see it**
Focus:	**Creating and accepting the teacher in role as Miss Nancy; acting on indirect instruction**

Teacher: Would you agree to let me become Miss Nancy in our drama? [They do]

Teacher sets out chair and puts the wooden box (open and not too close to the chair) on the floor.

When I put on this shawl and sit in this chair, I will become Miss Nancy but I will need you to help me so that we can all believe that Miss Nancy is here.

Teacher places the shawl around her shoulders and sits in the chair.

Teacher: I need your help to become Miss Nancy.
Who has some ideas about how Miss Nancy might sit?
Where might she have her hands?
Do her feet look right?

Students offer suggestions; teacher accepts and tries out until everyone agrees that this is what Miss Nancy looks like.

<u>Teacher (sitting in chair as Miss Nancy) narrates:</u>

It's been so wonderful getting to look at my old picture album again. It all happened so long ago and it is so hard to remember.

I guess that's what happens when you get old and you lose touch with your old friends.

I wonder if any of my old friends and family members have thought about me lately? It would be so good to hear from them again. Maybe their letters would help me to remember those special moments that we shared together so long ago.

Perhaps someone will bring me a letter that I can read and put in my memory box. Oh, all this remembering makes me tired! I think I'll take a little nap. [*Teacher closes eyes. Brief pause*]

<u>11. Moving the story along</u> — ***<u>1 minute</u>***

Grouping: **As above**
Strategy: **Narration**
Administration: **Shawl; chair; old small wooden box big enough for letters**
Focus: **Listening and moving silently**

Teacher stands up and removes the shawl. As s/he is doing so,

<u>Teacher narrates:</u> And so Miss Nancy waited for the mail to arrive. Each of her friends *had* written a letter and, while she was napping, each one had carefully crept in and deposited the letter in Miss Nancy's special memory box without waking her.

Teacher resumes seated position with the shawl and closes his/her eyes.

Teacher (as Miss Nancy), awakes and says:

My goodness! All this remembering makes me very sleepy. [*S/he nods off again*]

Note: The students should be able to read the clues in the narration above. They will individually creep up and put their letters in the wooden box. However, you may need to clarify with them what they are expected to do. If nothing happens,

Teacher (waking up) looks in his/her box and says sadly:

I was just dreaming that my memory box was full of letters that each one of my friends had written to me and that they had brought their letters and put them in my box. Oh dear! [*Teacher closes eyes*]

This should work. If not, come out of role by standing up and dropping your shawl and instructing this task openly. You might start by saying, "What do you think Miss Nancy is hoping will happen? Can we do that, do you think? How will we do that without waking Miss Nancy?" *You might even want to do a little practice demonstration, then resume the role.*

12. Reading the letters — ***5 minutes***

Grouping:	**As above**
Strategy:	**Teacher in role**
Administration:	**Letters in the memory box**
Focus:	**To hear each other's memories of an imaginary past**

Teacher (as Miss Nancy) wakes up and sees the memory box full of letters:

Oh, look. It's full of letters! My dreams were right! My friends haven't forgotten me. I wonder what they will say! [*Teacher reads individual letters and responds to the memories presented*]

Note: You will take the clues from the texts. You need not read each letter completely, but it is important that students hear Miss Nancy acknowledging their writing.

When the letter reading is over,

Teacher (as Miss Nancy):

This has been one of the happiest days for a long time. What a wonderful life I have had. And to think I was forgetting. I mustn't forget to thank my dear friends for helping me to remember!

Teacher moves away from chair, taking off the shawl and coming out of role.

Note: If the children have written a group letter, the teacher opens eyes, sees the letter and gets up slowly and moves to the letter and reads it aloud, taking clues from the text, as above. S/he then returns to the chair, removing shawl.

13. Story completion — ***3 minutes***

Grouping: **Whole Group**
Strategy: **Story reading**
Administration: **Text of *Wilfrid Gordon McDonald Partridge***
Focus: **Listening**

Teacher out of role: Well, the photos and the letters that Miss Nancy received in our story drama certainly helped her to remember. Now, let's hear what the author, Mem Fox, wrote in her story about how her Wilfrid Gordon McDonald Partridge found a way to help Miss Nancy remember.

Teacher reads from: ***So Wilfrid Gordon went home again to look for memories for Miss Nancy*** ... to the end of the story.

14. Creating our own memories — ***6–7 minutes***

Grouping: **Individual**
Strategy: **Drawing**
Administration: **Paper and crayons**
Focus: **Reflection**

Teacher: I wonder what we will remember about today's drama?

Let's all draw a picture that we can add to our memories about the time that we did a drama about Miss Nancy. It can be about anything that you want to remember about today, so that when you see it many years from now, you'll remember about our drama work and the story we created together.

15. Connecting the story to our own lives ***5 minutes***

Grouping:	**Whole Group**
Strategy:	**Discussion**
Administration:	**None**
Focus:	**Reflection**

These are some questions that you might like to consider as ways into helping the students reflect on the experience they have just shared:

I wonder why memories are so important in our lives?

How does this story connect with your own experiences?

How do memories change as people grow?

How can memories help us with our learning?

What is it that I really want to remember when I am older?

Materials

Activity 3: Sticky note paper; felts; chart paper
Activity 4 (Option): Four brown paper bags; 3 x 5 cards; felt markers
Activity 5: Text of *Wilfrid Gordon McDonald Partridge*
Activity 6: Antique picture album

Activity 7: Caption strips (4" x 36"); dark felt markers (one per group); shawl
Activity 8: Shawl to signify Miss Nancy
Activity 9: Paper and pencils
Activity 14: Paper and felts

Resources

Fox, M. (1984). *Wilfrid Gordon McDonald Partridge.* Toronto, ON: Puffin/Penguin Books.
Steichen, E. (1955). *The family of man.* Published for the Museum of Modern Art. New York, NY: Simon & Schuster.

Bibliography on the theme of intergenerational relationships

Bahr, M. (1992). *The memory box.* Illinois: Albert Whitman and Company.
Baker, J. (1980). *Millicent.* Great Britain: Andre Deutsch.
Brandenberg, A. (1979). *The two of them.* New York, NY: Mulberry Books.
Egger, B. (1986). *Marianne's grandmother.* New York, NY: Dutton.
Flournoy, V. (1987). *The patchwork quilt.* Toronto, ON: Penguin Books.
Gilman, P. (1992). *Something from nothing.* Richmond Hill, ON: NorthWinds Press.
McFarlane, S. (1993). *Waiting for the whales.* Victoria, BC: Orca Books.
Reynolds, M., & Smith-Ary, L. (2001). *A present for Mrs. Kazinski.* Victoria, BC: Orca Books.
Rylant, C. (1982). *When I was young in the mountains.* New York, NY: Penguin Books.
Spalding, A. (1999). *Me and Mr. Mah.* Victoria, BC: Orca Books.
Uchida, Y. (1994). *The wise old woman.* Don Mills, ON: Macmillan.
Watson, J. (1989). *Grandpa's slippers.* New York. NY: Scholastic.
Zagwyn-Turney, D. (1993). *Long Nellie.* Victoria, BC: Orca Books.

Chapter Four

New Boots for Winter

Based on *Those Shoes*, written by Maribeth Boelts and illustrated by Noah Jones

Why Did We Choose This Story?

We chose this story because it offers lots of opportunities for engaging with the complexities of communicating, making meaning in real and imagined worlds, and because:

- The family structure reflects a reality for many children; the protagonists are boys.
- It is about who has and who does not have; about a family in which "there is no room for 'want' … just 'need'" (Boelts, 2009, p. 2).
- It is about friendship and the appreciation of the needs of others.
- The story highlights aspects of consumerism where status in our society is often represented by possessions.
- In terms of direct curriculum application, the story offers many opportunities for numeracy, comparisons, dedicated vocabulary as well as an examination of the understanding of status and place.

Safford and Barrs (2005) note that "[t]here is no quick or simple transition from creative arts to literacy" (p. 199), and so this story drama structure has a number of preliminary strategies. As an introduction, we use the Mantle of the Expert (MoE) approach, an umbrella drama strategy that uses a variety of conventions and techniques to "release new capacities" (Bolton, 2003, p. 136) in students. The role that the students take on, while individually expressed, operates within a collective context and that context of "shoe designers" is always one of expertise in which students "function as adults in a world of employment". This role demands a different way of thinking, imagining and talking as they "build commitment through carefully arranged group tasks" (p. 129). MoE is designed not only to promote curriculum integration but also to provide a strong context for deep understanding.

Key Understandings and Questions

- What is the effect of advertising on the lives of young people?
- Status is often the result of what you have rather than who you are.

The following structure is organized in two parts, the first (Part 1) leading into the actual text of Those Shoes *provides a comprehensive, integrated unit of work, suitable for students, 10 years and older. Depending on your time, the curriculum context and the age/development of your students, you may choose to work only with Part 2, adapting the story drama structure as appropriate. Part 2 on its own, works well with younger grades and can take about one-and-half hours. Part 1 may be broken up into smaller units, but, if you use it as a whole, it should also take about one-and-half hours.*

PART I

1. If the shoe fits — *7 minutes*

Grouping: **Whole class seated in a circle**

Strategy: **Category game**

Administration: **None**

Focus: **To draw attention to shoes**

Teacher: Before we begin our drama today, we are going to play a game that will require you to think about your feet on your feet.

Everyone, line up on this side of the room. [They do]

Good.

I am going to call out a prompt and if it "fits", your task is to cross the floor. You'll need to listen carefully before you respond. For example, let's try this one:

- Cross the floor if your shoes have laces. [They do]

Good. Any problems?

Let's try another one:

- Cross the floor if your shoes close with Velcro
- … if your shoes are closed in some other way
- … if your shoes are slip-ons

You might ask the students to describe how their closings are different.

- Cross the floor if your shoes have open toes.
- … if your shoes have stripes
- … if your shoes have a logo
- … if you know the name of the manufacturer

Again, check for understanding.

- Cross the floor if your shoes are new in the last month
- … if your shoes belonged to someone before you
- … if they are a bit big for you
- … if they are feeling a bit tight
- … if you tried these shoes on in a store before you bought them

Great! Let's come back to the circle and just talk to the person beside you about your shoes and how many times they let you cross the floor. [They do]

They may want to share some of the differences between their shoes and identify those shoes that carry a logo and talk about what that logo represents.

If we were to put all your shoes in a pile, how would you know which shoes belonged to you? What is it about your shoes that would tell you that? [They discuss]

2. Setting the context — ***10 minutes***

Grouping:	**Pairs**
Strategy:	**Observation and discussion; Mantle of the Expert (MoE)**
Administration:	**A variety of shoes, one for each pair; chart to fill (Figure 1); pencils; rulers**
Focus:	**To understand what makes a shoe a shoe**

Teacher: We have spent some time thinking about our own shoes, now we are going to have a chance to look at a shoe that has been worn by someone else. But before we do that, we need to know what we are looking at and what we are looking for.

In order to do the next work, we are each going to take on a role.

I'd like you to imagine that you are an apprentice in a shoe design school, studying to be a shoe designer.

What might be some of the skills that you would need to learn if you were going to design shoes? [They suggest]

You might want to list these skills on chart paper or the board.

Teacher: In this drama, we are going to be the people who have chosen to come to this school to learn the trade of shoe design. What might be the name of our school?

Think carefully as we only time for a few suggestions. Of course, these will only be working names until we make it official. [They suggest and teacher lists]

Thank you. In order to get ready for our drama and our roles in it, what do you imagine the studio in which we work looks like? See our design studio in your mind's eye.

Given the time, students may collaborate on drawing a suggested design of the studio. What sorts of furniture might be used? What supplies would be handy? What sort of displays might there be, and so on. For further ideas and deeper experiences in MoE, see Heathcote & Bolton (1995).

Teacher: Now we are ready to begin our drama.

The teacher is now going to work in role. There is simply a slight shift in your position. You are no longer the school teacher, but, rather, the instructor of a class of young adults studying shoe design. You might want to signal this shift by picking up some papers or a clip board, adding a jacket or a pair of glasses, anything that makes you feel a bit different and that signals that difference to the students. They will begin to understand who they are in terms of their role and age by the way in which you address them.

Teacher in role: Designers, our task today is one that is extremely challenging. First, we need to remind ourselves of the fundamentals of shoe design. With your partner, please carefully examine the shoe that I am about to give you.

Teacher hands out shoes and continues,

Teacher in role: You will need to look very carefully. What are some of the things we might observe? [They offer laces, colours, closures and different things identified through the game]

Good! Of course, you will look at the outside but you will also need to look at the inside to see what you can learn. What do you see there? [They offer numbers, insoles, manufacturer's name …]

On this chart that I am giving you, there are a number of categories.

As the charts and rulers are being passed out,

Teacher in role: As you look at those categories, see if there are any that you don't know. [They discuss]

If there are questions, take them.

Teacher in role: Right, let's not waste any time but get to work. You have only a few minutes to learn as much as you can about this shoe and to get that information charted. Be sure you have all the equipment you might need to help you.

As you are working, you might like to think about the kind of person to whom the shoe might have belonged.

Students work collaboratively, charting and observing. Time allotted depends on their skills and engagement. When they are finished,

Teacher in role: Using your charts for reference,

- What qualities in these shoes would appeal to the buyers?
- What is it about these shoes that would have invited someone to purchase them? For example, style? colour? comfort? Of course, as designers, we are always looking for that special quality that will "grab" the public. [They work/discuss]
- What special qualities do we need to pay attention to? I think we might list them here as references for our next design project. [They share, teacher or student may list]

Let's come out of role for a moment and check in.

How is this all working for you? [Brief discussion]

It is not always necessary to do a check-in, but if it is new way of working, it may be helpful for the students to share.

3. The ultimate shoe **_15 minutes_**

Grouping:	**Pairs as before; groups of four**
Strategy:	**Designing**
Administration:	**Blank paper; pencils; coloured felts**
Focus:	**To begin to think as designers**

Teacher in role: Now for the challenge I spoke of earlier. Because of the skills you have demonstrated and your design expertise, the director of shoe development has decided to give you a once in a lifetime opportunity. You could become the next designers to capture the youth shoe market.

Keeping in mind the ideas that we have just discussed, our task is to create "the" shoe for the next decade. Remember, it has to appeal to a wide audience of students: the 8–13-year-old market. Think back to when you were that age and what you liked; the shoe that you hoped to have and that you wanted to wear every day. Remember, this is your opportunity to shine as designers.

As paper is distributed,

Teacher in role: Use pencils to begin with and with your partner, sketch out your ideas before you choose your colours. These first drafts are important and will give us the range of ideas for us to use later. [Students sketch for no more than four minutes]

As students work, encourage discussion and sharing of ideas and suggestions.

Teacher in role: As you know, this company is grounded in the idea of collaborative design.

As you work together, you might wish to create a name for your shoe; for example, *The Flyer* and, if you are up for it, create a special mark—a logo—that would identify this shoe for the youth market.

These two tasks (and the one below) are designed to provide quick finishers with further tasks that matter.

<u>**Teacher in role:**</u>	If you are truly inspired, the marketing division would be happy to hear any marketing phrases, such as with *The Flyer: Catch the Air!* When you are finished, just bring your designs to me and I will see that they are displayed for the director's consideration.

Designs can be used for portfolio assessment, displayed for observation/discussion.

<u>***4. Walking in those shoes*** — ***4 minutes***</u>

Grouping:	**Individual**
Strategy:	**Movement**
Administration:	**Tambourine**
Focus:	**To explore feelings of status**

<u>**Teacher in role:**</u>	Having just begun our designs of the "ultimate" shoe, there is something that we have not yet considered: What is it about these shoes that will make someone feel proud to wear them? How can we generate the psychological appeal of desire? We have been focusing on the visual impact of our designs but we know that advertising and marketing are as much about the feelings that the product evokes in the wearer as they are about the words and the pictures. Our competitors are working with new ideas around product development. The director is anxious for us to

explore other ways of understanding the buyers whom we wish to attract. We've been working with our heads and our hands and now we need to take that understanding into our bodies.

Everyone, please stand and find a place to work on your own. [They do]

Imagine that you are a young person and the new owner of those shoes that everyone wants. You are heading off to school in your new shoes. Let's see how your shoes make you feel as you walk to meet your friends at school.

Take a moment to feel those shoes on your feet and when you hear the signal, begin to walk. Be careful not to bump into anyone; respect everyone's space. [They do. Note: some designs may generate different kinds of movement]

Using a signal on the tambourine,

Teacher in role: Stop, everyone. Remember that feeling of ownership.

Again, respecting everyone's space, this time walk as if the shoes on your feet are not like the shoes that everyone else is wearing. How do you feel about that? How does that change how you walk down the street? [They do]

After a minute, stop everyone with the signal again.

Teacher in role: Thank you. It was really clear for me to see how your feelings and your walk were affected by what you were thinking. As designers what might be useful to us in our marketing promotion, from that experience?

Just talk to the person beside you about the differences between wearing the shoes that everyone has and having shoes that are not like everyone else's.
[They do]

Let's share some of our ideas and feelings about that.
[They do]

In this discussion, keep the focus on the possibilities of both written and visual promotion. Asking "How might we word that idea?" "What might we see on a poster?" The possibilities for further design (visual art) and marketing (writing) are many, but we would suggest that you engage with the story and then revisit the activities above.

5. Transitioning into the story **4 minutes**

Grouping: **Whole class**
Strategy: **Story reading**
Administration: **Text of *Those Shoes***
Focus: **To listen**

Teacher in role: We have begun to uncover some of the issues that face us all, not just young people. Consumerism affects everyone and we depend on companies that make the goods that they be honest in their advertising.

We are going to leave our roles as shoe designers to work in another way.

Come out of character, perhaps by removing glasses, a slight shift in voice or moving to a different position.

PART 2

If you choose to begin here, we suggest that you use Activity 1 (If the shoe fits) as a way in.

6. Delving into the story **4 minutes**

Grouping: **Whole class**
Strategy: **Story reading**
Administration: **Text of *Those Shoes***
Focus: **To listen**

If students have explored Part 1, begin here:

Teacher: The story that we are about to explore, *Those Shoes*, highlights the pressures on young people to belong, to wear the right clothes, have the right gear. What might be some of the things that everyone wants? [They tell]

If students have not done Part 1, we suggest the following:

Teacher: Let's have a look at the cover. What do you see in this picture? What do you think the story might be about? What in the picture tells you that? [They respond]

Good! You are thinking like authors.

Let's hear how our author begins our story.

Teacher reads: ***I have dreams about those shoes*** … to … ***Next, Allen Jacoby and Terrence each get a pair.***

7. Picture this! **10 minutes**

Grouping: **Groups of five**
Strategy: **Tableau**
Administration: **None**
Focus: **To embody thoughts and feeling in stillness**

Teacher: Please move into groups of five. [They do]

We are going to interpret what we just heard by working in tableaux—creating visual images with our bodies.

In your groups, we will see five students somewhere in the school—gymnasium getting ready for the game; in the classroom; lining up for lunch; on the playground; in the lunchroom or some other place in the school that might be more suitable for your ideas that would serve as an interesting background for an image.

This picture will show a group of students at school at a moment in time. All of them will be wearing the popular shoes except for one. What might the students be doing? Create a still picture that shows how we are feeling but without moving or speaking.

This is not a formal school picture but a picture in which we see the students frozen as they are *doing* something. Any questions?

Your picture can make it easy for all of us to know who is not wearing the right shoes. Or you can be very subtle and make us work to figure it out.

You don't have a lot of time—say three minutes—so get to work.

Students may need more time and, if so, provide it. When students appear ready,

Teacher: We will now see these drafts for what they can tell us about how each person in the tableau feels or thinks about what is happening.

Which group would like to begin? [A group offers] Thank you.

While the first group gets ready, we will close our eyes. When the group is ready, I will count down, three-two-one and say "open". The group will be frozen and we will be able to look carefully at it to see how the people in the group are feeling.

*You may wish to see these tableaux one following the other without comment or to stop after each one for discussion. Or you may want to use Option 7a to extend the tableau work. If not, move to **

OPTION

7a. Discovering what lies beneath the picture ***5 minutes***

Grouping:	**As above**
Strategy:	**Tapping in**
Administration:	**None**
Focus:	**To express thoughts in role**

You may wish to work with one or two groups or with every group.

Teacher: Just hold your tableau. I am going to come around and when you feel my hand on your shoulder, just speak as the person in the tableau, the thought that is in your mind.

Be sure to leave your hand on the student's shoulder for the time he or she is speaking. Don't rush this. Sometimes a student won't speak. Just wait until you are sure that nothing is coming and then move on without comment.

You do not need to ask every member of the tableau to speak. Remind students that they only need to say a few words. The lifting of your hand is also a signal that they can stop speaking.

Teacher may invite students observing to contribute to the questions. They may want to tap in themselves or they may prefer you to tap in using their questions.

Some examples:

- What's on the menu that you are going to eat?
- How important are your shoes to your game?
- How long have you all been friends?
- Apart from school, what kinds of things do you do together?

* Thank you. We are beginning to get an idea of the students in this school. Let's move on to the next group and see what they will add to our understanding.

Continue until all groups have been seen (and heard).

<u>**Teacher:**</u> Isn't it interesting how powerful those images can be and how much they can tell us?

Let's listen again to the story to find out more about Jeremy and his friends at school.

<u>***8. Shopping for shoes*** ***3 minutes***</u>

Grouping: **Whole class**

Strategy: **Teacher narration; movement**

Administration: **Text of *Those Shoes***

Focus: **To listen and experience**

<u>**Teacher reads from:**</u> ***Then one day, in the middle of kickball*** … to … ***"How exciting!" Grandma says. "What size are they?"***

For younger students with little or no experience of improvisation:

<u>**Teacher:**</u> For the next part of our drama, would you all agree to be Jeremy and try on those shoes? [They agree]

Close your eyes and imagine those shoes in front of you. Just about brand new! Can you see them, those black high tops? You are going to have to work very hard as you try on those imaginary shoes.

First the right foot. Ease your foot in and tie up the laces. You can do it! [They do]

Now the other foot. [They do]

Done! Stand up and just take a moment to admire those shoes. [They do]

Begin to walk around the store. You may see a mirror and might like to admire those shoes for a moment. Keep moving and feeling your feet inside those shoes. [They do]

Oh, oh! Something's not quite right. Toes are starting to feel a little "crunched". Keep moving but be aware that your toes are not comfortable. Oooh! Try stretching your toes out inside your shoes; maybe that will help? They are perfect … except for how they feel.

As students try out the shoes, offer the above as prompts responding to what you see happening.

But by tomorrow they will be GREAT!

For older students who are comfortable with improvising:

OPTION

9. Hoping they fit ***5 minutes***

Grouping:	**Pairs**
Strategy:	**Improvisation**
Administration:	**None**
Focus:	**To predict**

Teacher: Now, we have an opportunity to write a bit of the story for ourselves. In drama, we call this improvisation. We make it up but we do so on the basis of what we know. Find a partner. [They do]

As you will be Grandma; Bs you will be Jeremy. We are going to set the scene at the thrift store. Thinking as playwrights, what do you think the conversation might be about? How do you imagine this scene might turn out? Will the shoes fit? Will Grandma buy them for Jeremy? Remember what Grandma said earlier, "There's no room for 'want' around here—just 'need.'"

We will discover what happens as we see Jeremy trying on those shoes and his conversation with his Grandma as he does so.

We are improvising and so we need to do a couple of things to get ready:

First, find a space with your partner. [They do]

Decide together: Will someone be sitting? Who has the shoes? Who will speak the first line? Decide together what it might be. [They do]

Depending upon the confidence and the ability of the students, it may be useful to solicit ideas for a first line; otherwise:

Teacher: We are going to try that out now. Does everybody have a good idea of how we are going to begin? This is not a long scene but we will have an idea of how things turn out. [They improvise]

It is helpful if you move around to listen, to provide encouragement and to pick up ideas that you may wish to comment on.

So, how did your scene go? What happened? What ideas came up? [They tell]

Depending upon the group and the time, some may wish to show just the final few lines and action.

10. The internal argument — ***6 minutes***

Grouping:	**Whole class**
Strategy:	**Story reading**
Administration:	**Text of *Those Shoes***
Focus:	**To experience the power of want**

Teacher: Thank you. Have a seat and let's hear how the author writes that scene.

Teacher reads from: ***My heart is pounding hard as I take off my shoes*** … to … ***Grandma gives me a hug.***

Just talk to your partner about how what you have just done was different or similar to what happens in the story. [They do]

Teacher continues reading:

I check every day, but those shoes don't stretch ... to ... ***That night I am awake for a long time thinking about Antonio.***

11. Lying awake — ***5 minutes***

Grouping:	**Individual**
Strategy:	**Writing in role**
Administration:	**Paper and pencils for everyone**
Focus:	**To explore what keeps Jeremy awake**

Teacher: You know what it is like when you can't sleep—so many thoughts going around and around in your head. Some of them don't make any sense at all, and some of them make too much sense.

Beginning to think as Jeremy in bed, quietly find your own space and imagine what those thoughts might be as

I hand you paper and pencil. Don't talk to anyone; these are your private thoughts on this night. What's keeping you awake? Just let the words flow onto the paper without worrying about punctuation or spelling—it's called stream of consciousness—the words are streaming from your mind onto the page. [They write]

They will need anywhere from five to seven minutes to gather and write their thoughts.

12. Thinking about Antonio ***5 minutes***

Grouping: **Whole group**

Strategy: **Conscience alley**

Administration: **A pair of running shoes (they need to be in good condition)**

Focus: **To hear the thinking of Jeremy**

Teacher: Just put your pencils down now. Don't bother about finishing a sentence. Read over those thoughts of yours and still thinking as Jeremy, underline the words or phrase that best expresses what's in your mind this night. [They do]

Please commit that phrase or sentence to memory. [They do]

Will someone volunteer to take on the role of becoming Jeremy? You won't have to say anything yet but only listen carefully. [Someone volunteers]

Thank you. The rest of you make two lines, leaving enough room for Jeremy to walk slowly between you. As Jeremy moves down this line, each person will say the sentence or phrase that best tells us what you are thinking about tonight. Only one person speaks at a time so that Jeremy's thoughts can be heard. Any questions?

Sometimes students are a little confused, especially if they have not worked with this strategy before. Clear up any difficulties before you begin.

Teacher: Perhaps it would help to make it more real for all of us if you carried these?

Teacher hands a pair of running shoes to the volunteer, "Jeremy".

Remember, Jeremy, walk slowly enough so that you hear every thought. [S/he does]

When "Jeremy" reaches the end of the alley,

Teacher: Thank you. This is a young man with a lot on his mind.

Turn to the person next to you and talk about that experience. [They do]

"Jeremy", you had your own thoughts. What did you hear that expressed the same ideas?

Just sit down where you are and listen to the end of the story. [They do]

13. Doing the right thing ***1 minute***

Grouping: **Whole group**
Strategy: **Story reading**
Administration: **Text of *Those Shoes***
Focus: **To hear the end of the story**

Teacher reads from: ***When morning comes, I try on my shoes one last time …*** to the end of the story.

14. The real in the pretend ***As long as needed***

Grouping:	**Whole group**
Strategy:	**Reflection**
Administration:	**None**
Focus:	**To move towards new understanding**

Teacher: This was a powerful story that drew us all in. Just turn to the person next to you and talk about your experiences working in this story drama.

What, I wonder, does this story say about friendship?

Depending upon what the students have just done in the drama (Part 1, Part 2 or both), the following questions will act as prompts for reflection:

Teacher: How might your work as shoe designers inform your thinking about the story?

Let's leave our roles as shoe designers and speak from our own experiences. What connections do you make to this story?

What examples can you suggest where advertising plays a large role in our lives?

I wonder why it is that what we have or wear becomes such an important part of our lives?

Those Shoes is a story about consumerism, about buying things—things that we need, things that we just want. I wonder when it is right for us to receive things that we may not need but do want?

Extensions

If you are moving on to do a unit on social justice issues, you might like to introduce the concept of ethical practices in manufacturing, child labour, working conditions and the growing awareness of the power of advertising and marketing on young people. The promotion of consumerism targeting children is becoming an international concern.

"Social research company, Australia Scan, says the 'tween' market (which covers 7–13 year olds) is worth more than $10 billion in Australia. Anywhere between $250 million and $1 billion of this is spent on clothing" (Rush & La Nauze, 2006).

And/or you might like to use the following as a poster:

> According to the Commission for Children and Young People (Australia, 2011), "it is estimated the average child sees more than 40,000 television ads a year. Advertisers spend more than $12 billion per year targeting the youth market because of its strong contribution to the consumer economy. According to one estimate in the United States, children aged 14 and under make $24 billion in direct purchases and influence $190 billion in family purchases."

Materials

Activity 2: A variety of shoes, one for each pair of students (these may be acquired by shopping in your own closet or by visiting a thrift shop); copies of chart (Figure 1); pencils; rulers
Activity 3: Blank paper; pencils; coloured felts
Activity 4: Tambourine
Activity 5: Text of *Those Shoes*
Activity 6: Text of *Those Shoes*
Activity 8: Text of *Those Shoes*
Activity 10: Text of *Those Shoes*
Activity 11: Paper and pencils
Activity 12: A pair of running shoes
Activity 13: Text of *Those Shoes*

Resources

Boelts, M. (2007). *Those shoes*. Somerville, MA: Candlewick Press.
Commission for Children and Young People and Child Guardian. (2011). Fact sheet 4. Retrieved from http://www.publicguardian.qld.gov.au/__data/assets/pdf_file/0019/263260/Corporate-Fact-Sheet4.pdf
Gladwell, M. (2001). The coolhunt. In D. Remnick (Ed.), *Life stories: Profiles from The New Yorker* (pp. 468–481). New York, NY: The Modern Library.
Rush, E., & La Nauze, A. (2006). Corporate paedophilia: Sexualization of children in Australia. Discussion paper (Australia Institute), no.90. Retrieved from http://www.tai.org.au/documents/dp_fulltext/DP90.pdf

A SHOE DESCRIPTION	
Observation	**Information**
1. MAKE OF SHOE	
2. TYPE OF SHOE	
3. COLOUR OF SHOE	
4. SHAPE OF TOE	
5. TYPE OF HEEL	
6. CLOSURE	
7. INSOLE INFORMATION	
8. MARKINGS: inside/outside	
9. LOGO	
10. SIZE	
11. Using the ruler, measure the length of the shoe.	
12. Using the ruler, measure the width of the shoe at its widest point.	

NAME (print)	DATE	SIGNATURE
____________	____________	____________

Figure 1: A shoe description for Activity 2. May be photocopied for classroom use. © 2016 *Into the Story 2: More Stories! More Drama!* by Carole Miller and Juliana Saxton. Bristol, UK: Intellect.

Chapter Five

I'm Too Old for a Trike Now

Based on *Tricycle,* written by Elisa Amado and illustrated by Alfonso Ruano

Why Did We Choose This Story?

We chose this story for its open approach to difficult issues that are raised through the story of three children. Margarita lives in a "great big house"; a hedge divides it from the "small shack" next door where Rosario and Chepe live.

- This story offers the potential to broaden awareness of another culture and for integration with social s tudies. It presents a world in which rich and poor can and do live side by side.
- Although the storytelling is direct and the words are easily comprehended, the text itself is often ambiguous and metaphorical. These same qualities are reflected in the enchanting illustrations.
- Told from the perspective of a child, the writing has a sense of innocence with an underlying subtext that suggests there is something ominous in what, on the surface, appears to be an idyllic environment. From an adult point of view, we glimpse the political instability and class consciousness that is an inherent theme of the text.
- The story looks at the universals of rich and poor, "haves" and "have nots", and the opportunities afforded those for whom money is not an issue.
- It deals with themes of friendship and the responsibilities that are a part of those relationships.
- It raises the ambiguities of truth-telling and begins to consider the implications of what is ethical behaviour.

Key Understandings and Questions

- There are times in life when issues of right and wrong become blurred.
- The world is not black and white and yet, for children, it can seem to be so.
- There are many incidents in young lives that, on reflection, we can see to be life-changing.

1. Keeping or taking? — *15 minutes*

Grouping: **Whole group, sitting in a horseshoe**

Strategy: **Game: Keeper of the Keys**

Administration: **Large, open space; blindfold; set of keys; rolled up newspaper; a chair with enough chairs for class in a horseshoe; OR class in a horseshoe sitting on the floor; jar with class names to facilitate choosing participants**

Focus: **Entering the drama world**

Teacher: Before we begin our drama, we are going to play a game that provides us with a beginning for our drama. To start, I will put this chair in front of you and place this set of keys near the chair.

Teacher places the chair a few feet from the ends of the horseshoe.

Teacher: The name of this game is Keeper of the Keys. Is there someone who would like to be that Keeper? [A volunteer is selected]

Keeper, your job is to guard the keys. This roll of newspaper can be used to ward off anyone who tries to take them. The challenge for you is that you will not be able to see who is sneaking up, so you will have to listen very, very carefully. Are you still

willing to undertake this responsibility?
[Keeper agrees]

Thank you. Come and sit in the chair and I will blindfold you. [*Teacher does so*] And here is your instrument to ward off any intruders. [*Hands student the roll of newspaper*]

Who would like to come and try to steal the keys? Remember, you must do so without making any noise that might alert the Keeper. Who's willing to try?
[Student volunteers]

Keeper, if at any point, you think someone is close enough to get the keys, you must tap the intruder with your roll and he or she will be "out".

Group, your job is to be very quiet. Try not to disturb the action.

Note: If it is possible to dim the lights, Teacher can do so to enhance the tension.

Teacher: Are we all ready to begin? [They play]

Well done! Who else would like to have a try?

Students enjoy this game and may want to play it indefinitely! Limit the game to three or four tries.

Variations

- Each time, the tension will be enhanced if the keys are placed in a different position; i.e., start by placing the keys in front or at the side of the Keeper. For the last round, place them under the chair.
- Change the "intruders" each time. The Keeper may need more than one turn to build skill.

Teacher: What were some of the strategies we used to try and get by the Keeper? [They offer]

What makes that game so much fun? [They offer]

So, who was having the most fun? The Keeper? The taker? Or the watchers? [They suggest]

I think now we are ready to move on.

2. Temptation ***10 minutes***

Grouping: **Individual**

Strategy: **Discussion; listing**

Administration: **White board; pen**

Focus: **To move into the issues of the story**

Teacher: I wonder if there is anyone here who has lost something special? [Students offer]

What might be some of the words you would use to describe those feelings when you discover it is lost? [*Teacher records*] This is an interesting list and these words will play a part in our story.

Sometimes we lose things and sometimes things are taken from us without our knowing. I wonder what might cause people to take something that didn't belong to them? Let's hear some of your thinking. [They respond]

I wonder what is the difference between needing something and wanting it? [They discuss]

You've made some interesting distinctions about those different ways of looking at things.

The teacher may want to honour those contributions by including them in a summary.

Teacher: Let's come back now to our drama space on the floor. [They do]

I think we are ready now for our story.

3. Into the story ***5 minutes***

Grouping: **Whole class**

Strategy: **Reading aloud**

Administration: **Text of *Tricycle;* OHP or other media of page five with the volcano in the background**

Focus: **To provide the context and deepen engagement**

Teacher: Everything we've done so far will help us to understand the story drama for today. Our story is called *Tricycle* by Elisa Amado.

I remember my first tricycle, it was red and pretty important in my life. Who here remembers having something that belonged to them and was special? [Students share memories]

Students may talk about things they felt a sense of ownership for, and/or how they might have had to share with another family member.

Thank you. Those memories will help us enter the story today because it takes place far away from here, in a country in Central America. It is a story about children around your age (OR somewhat younger than you).

Let's look at the first picture and see what may be different from where we live. [*Teacher shows picture with volcano on p. 5; short discussion on those differences follows*]

I'm going to begin to read now. Listen to how the author describes the story's setting.

<u>**Teacher reads from:**</u> *(p. 5)* ***I walk outside in my bare feet*** … to *(p. 11)* … ***and goes back to work.*** [*Showing the pictures that accompany the text*]

What do we know about Margarita? [They discuss]

<u>**Teacher continues from:**</u> *(p. 12)* ***On the other side of the hedge*** … to … ***lunch every day.*** [*Showing the pictures of Rosario's house (pp. 12 & 13)*]

What does this picture tell us about their life? How might it be different from Margarita's life? [They discuss]

<u>**Teacher reads from:**</u> *(p. 15)* ***Right below the tree*** … to *(p. 16)* … ***Rosario climbs in from the other side and hides with me.***

4. Playing together — ***10 minutes***

Grouping: **Groups of three**
Strategy: **Tableau**
Administration: **None**
Focus: **To see the children at play**

<u>**Teacher:**</u> I wonder how a camera would capture the relationship of these three children when they play? We're going to see still pictures (or tableaux) of the children. It could be like a photo album. What kinds of things might they be doing? Let's hear some of your ideas. [They offer]

You have some interesting ideas. Now, get into groups of three. Each of you will be one of the children: Margarita, Rosario or Chepe. Remember, in drama, boys can play girls and vice versa.

Teacher can assign groups or they may be self-selected.

Teacher: You don't have much time, so you will have to work quickly. You may use any ideas that we've heard, but, of course, you may decide on something else. [Students work for approximately three minutes]

In a moment, we are going to be looking at these photographs as if we were looking through the pages of a photo album. And because this is drama, the picture can come alive so that we can hear what the children are saying as they play. So you need to think about the photo you have chosen to show us and what each of the children might be saying. Any questions about that new task?

If there are questions, address them. If not,

Teacher: How will what we say keep the author's intent?

You have two minutes to decide on your dialogue. [Students work]

We are going to see these tableaux as if we were turning the pages of a photograph album and when you hear me say "action", we will hear the lines of dialogue. When I say, "thank you", the groups may dissolve and sit down. We will see and hear each tableau without any comment.

As you are watching and listening, think about what these pictures tell us about their friendship.

After the tableaux are shared,

Teacher: What do we now know about these children, the kinds of things they do together, and how they play together? [They share]

Notice how clearly the pictures helped us to know a little more about them.

What do we now know about their relationship that the story hasn't told us?

Listen and accept what is said without judgment.

5. Back to the story — ***2 minutes***

Grouping:	**Whole class**
Strategy:	**Reading aloud**
Administration:	**Text of *Tricycle***
Focus:	**To introduce foreshadowing**

Teacher: Now that we know a little more, let's get back to our story.

Teacher reads from: *(p. 19)* ***Up in my tree*** … to … ***I hope fire doesn't fall on us from the sky.***

I wonder what in our lives could pose a threat to disturb our peace? [They discuss]

There are many things in life that can disturb us. Listen, as I continue:

Teacher repeats: ***Up in my tree, I can feel the north wind blowing and it is a little bit cold.*** Follow with: *(p. 20)* ***I hear Chepe's voice and look down*** … to *(p. 23)* ***Where's your trike" she scolds?*** [Omit "I don't know."]

6. Trying to explain — ***15 minutes***

Grouping:	**Pairs**
Strategy:	**Improvising dialogue**
Administration:	**None**
Focus:	**To explore how Margarita explains herself**

Teacher: Let's find out how Margarita explains to her mother about her trike. For the next part of our drama, we will be playwrights. We are going to create the conversation between Margarita and her mother (or her father, if you would prefer)—in drama it really doesn't matter. What is important is that we make this conversation believable.

Make a pair with the person next to you and find a place to work on your own, so that you are not interfering with another pair. [They do]

Decide who will be the mother or father and who will be Margarita. [They decide]

Margaritas, raise your hand. Mothers/Fathers, raise yours. [They do]

Good! Now, as authors, you will need to make some decisions to help the scene. We know our roles but where will our scene take place? Will it take place inside or outside? [They decide]

It's very important that we a have a sense of location when improvising.

How many of you plan to be inside the house. [They indicate] Will you be sitting or standing? If you plan to sit, find your chair. If you are outside, what can you see? The hedge, perhaps?

Share what you see with your partner. Negotiate a common place. We can use those reference points to help us build belief in what we are doing. [They do]

Now, listen very carefully. [*Be sure that all are attending*]

We know from our story that Margarita's mother will speak first. Does anyone remember what she says and how she says it? [Someone may offer]

Now, here is the challenge: We don't know how Margarita is going to respond. Will Margarita tell the truth and, if so, what might her mother say or do? Or will she say something else and how might her mother respond to that? Perhaps the words we listed on the board will help you to think about your answer. Now, we know the first line of the scene: Mother says, "Where is your trike?" We even know how she says it!

You will need to plan carefully because it will help you to decide how the scene will be played. In this scene there will be three exchanges: (1) *Mother*, (2) *Margarita* and (3) *Mother.* If there is something else you want to say or do to help you end your scene, you may try it.

Note: Rather than taking questions, it may be better to say,

<u>Teacher:</u> I'll be around to help with any questions you may have. You are going to have to work quickly.

Remember, it is often easier to create a scene if you act it out as you plan.

As the students are working, teacher circulates and responds as necessary. When most appear to be ready, signal "One more minute."

<u>Teacher:</u> You've all been working really hard. I think you are ready to give your scene a try. We will rehearse this all together.

There will be lots of people speaking at once. In your pairs, you will really need to focus on one another and block out everyone else. This will take a lot of concentration.

When you have finished your scene just sit down and then I will know when everyone is done.

Take your places. I'll count down: three, two, one, action. [They improvise]

Thank you. Just talk about how that went with your partner and if there is anything you want to change or improve. We have time to try it again. [They do]

If the students want to do another rehearsal, give them the opportunity.

Teacher: Ah, there are some very interesting scenes being created. Let's see and hear some of these dialogues. We were playwrights and now we are going to be both actors *and* audience. They are all important roles in the theatre.

As we watch, we'll listen to hear the different kinds of explanations and responses from Margarita and her mother. Focus on how real these scenes sound.

Is there a pair that would like to start us off? [A pair volunteers]

Thank you. The rest of us will just sit down where we are and watch your scene. Just be sure you can all see.

Note: There is no need to set up a performance area. This is an informal sharing and in the interests of time and clarity, it is better for students to perform where they have been used to practicing.

Teacher hears some or all pairs, depending upon the willingness of the class and the time available. After the sharing,

Teacher: It was so interesting to hear the different ways in which Margarita responded to her mother.

At this point, if you are working with a class just learning how to work in role, you might like to say, "Let's stop here for a moment and think about what we've seen and heard. What was it that made these scenes real for you?" "If we were going to re-play these scenes, what changes might you make to help us believe in the situation between Margarita and her mother?" *This can be a way to build criteria for role playing with your students. It is also another way to develop the drama contract. Or, you can just move on,*

Now let's hear what Margarita says to her mother in our author's version of the story.

Teacher repeats: *(p. 23)* ***Where's your trike? she scolds*** … and adds, ***I don't know, I say*** and continues reading to *(p. 27)* … ***lie there waiting for footsteps to come.***

7. Under the bed — ***10 minutes***

Grouping: **Individual**

Strategy: **Writing in role**

Administration: **Paper and pencil**

Focus: **To explore Margarita's thinking**

Teacher: Imagine that you are Margarita as she sits in her room. I wonder what you are thinking and feeling? You know what really happened. I wonder why you didn't tell your mother the truth? You saw what happened to your trike.

I wonder if you lied to protect your friends or to protect yourself? You need to think about that.

Take out a piece of paper and a pencil. You are going to write a note to your mother about this event. What is it that you want her to know? What's on your mind? What are you frightened of? What are you thinking and feeling? What do you need to say to her?

Note: When students are writing in role, they will often stop writing because they think they have run out of ideas. If the teacher says something like, "I see some people have stopped writing to do some more thinking" that will often prompt them to start writing again. Usually five minutes is enough time, depending on the students' facility as writers. Try not to rush them.

Teacher:	Finish up now. Please read over what you have written. When you have done so, choose the sentence that you feel would tell your mother most clearly what it is that you would like her to understand about what happened today. Underline that sentence or phrase. [They do] You will need to remember it for our next activity.

8. What will the mother hear? 7 minutes

Grouping:	**Whole class divided into two lines; a volunteer to be Margarita**
Strategy:	**Conscience alley**
Administration:	**The mother's shawl**
Focus:	**To hear Margarita's thinking**

Teacher:	Sometimes it is difficult to say what we are thinking but in this part of our drama, we can create a special space where we can speak our thoughts aloud. With a partner, come and stand here [*indicating a place in the room*] and create two lines, facing each other. Leave enough space for someone to walk between you. [They do] This strategy is called Conscience Alley because we will be hearing the thoughts and feelings of Margarita. Now, before we begin, we will need someone to be the mother to hear those thoughts. Who will volunteer to take on the role of the mother? You don't have to speak but to listen very hard to what is

being said as you move slowly down the line. [Student volunteers]

Come and stand at the beginning of our alley. [Student does so]

As her mother moves slowly down the alley you make for her, we will hear the thoughts that are going through Margarita's mind and what it is she really wants her mother to know. Everyone will have an opportunity to speak. So, Mother, you need to move slowly so that you and we can hear each individual comment.

There are many different thoughts that we experience when we are troubled so we need to be sure that we can hear everything that is being said. Does anyone have any questions before we begin?

Sometimes students are a little confused, especially if they have not worked with this strategy before. Clear up the difficulties before you begin so that the power of the feelings is not interrupted.

Teacher: Mother, would it help to wear this shawl? [Student decides] This is an opportunity for Margarita to tell her mother the kinds of things that are on her mind. Let's begin.

If there are problems as the strategy moves along, stop it quietly and sort it out. Then ask the student in role as the mother to begin again. After the walk is over,

Teacher: Sit down where you are. Take a moment to talk about what you heard that was unexpected or that confirmed what you were thinking and feeling. Mother, you will need to think about what you have just heard, as well. [They reflect]

After a minute or so of reflecting,

Teacher:	Turn to the person next to you and share your experience during this part of our drama. [They do] Let's share some of the things that were in our minds as we talked together. [They do] Thank you.

OPTION

We offer the following as an alternative to Conscience Alley.

8a. What will Mother hear? 7 minutes

Grouping:	**Whole group**
Strategy:	**Tapping in/Voice collage**
Administration:	**Students' writing**
Focus:	**To listen to a wide range of thoughts, feelings and ideas**

Teacher:	Close your eyes. I am going to move among you. When you feel my hand on your shoulder, speak the words you have underlined, aloud. We are building collective understanding and so we need to hear everyone's voice clearly. When you have finished, lower your head so that I know that you have spoken.

Teacher moves through the room randomly. Leave your hand on the student's shoulder until s/he has finished speaking. A firm but gentle touch encourages speech.

After the students have contributed, the teacher needs to leave some space for silent reflection (30–60 seconds).

Teacher:	Talk quietly to the person next to you about what you heard. [They do]

Who has something they would like to share?
[*This is an optional question and depends on the buzz of talk*]

9. The unwritten scene ***10 minutes***

Grouping:	**Whole class in role as Rosario and Chepe**
Strategy:	**Teacher in role as Juanita, Rosario and Chepe's mother; improvisation**
Administration:	**Large, old cardboard box; shawl for Juanita**
Focus:	**To confront the issues of the stolen tricycle**

Teacher narrates: The next day, Rosario's mother, Juanita, was looking for a box in which to take some chickens to market. She came upon the tricycle that her children had hidden under the box behind the shack.

Teacher: For the next part of our drama, we are all going to be in role. Would you all be willing to take on the roles of Rosario and her brother, Chepe? [They agree]

Will you accept me as their mother, Juanita? [They agree] When Juanita is talking to you as if you were her children, anyone can respond in role; more than one person can respond because you may have lots of different ideas. Just be sure that you listen to each other. We are not planning this scene; we are creating it all together as we are doing it.

You have already been actors so you know that it takes concentration and imagination to believe in the roles we are playing.

Our scene will take place when Rosario and Chepe's mother, Juanita, has just found the box under which her children have hidden the trike. Let's use this old cardboard box to help us believe as we build our scene.

Teacher moves to the drama space, placing a large cardboard box as if it were covering the trike. To begin the scene, lift the box up, look at what is revealed and then,

Teacher in role (calling): Rosario, Chepe, where are you? Come here at once! [*Teacher motions students over to join her*]

Look what I just found? Where did it come from? What is it doing here? I want an answer at once. And I want the truth! [Students begin to tell their versions]

*If students tell the truth, skip to *. If they prevaricate,*

Teacher in role: Don't think you can fool me! I'm pretty sure I've seen this trike before on the other side of the hedge. In fact, I'm sure Margarita rode over on it the other day when she came to get the tortillas with her mother! [They try to explain]

Listen and try not to interrupt as they give you their explanations. When they seem to have run out of words or they are beginning to repeat themselves,

Teacher in role: But you children get along so well. Why did you take it and why have you hidden it here? [Another chance to explain]

How much time you need for this strategy will depend on what is available to you and upon the responses of the children. Teacher in role provides an opportunity to challenge the children's thinking in order to make them think more deeply about the issues in the scene. When it feels right, conclude with,

Teacher in role: * You must return it right away.

How are you going to explain yourselves? After all, we may be poor but we are not thieves! [*This implication comes directly from the text (see p. 25)*]

Out of role. Thank you.

10. Figuring out choices and consequences — ***As long as necessary***

Group: **Whole class**

Strategy: **Reflection**

Administration: **Text of *Tricycle***

Focus: **To begin to think about when "the rules" may not apply**

Teacher (*if appropriate*): Well! That was pretty tense at times.

We have just created another scene in this story by hearing from the other side of the hedge and I wonder if anyone has anything they would like to say about that scene or about the story itself? [*They may or may not offer but it is another chance to build criteria*]

I wonder what motivates us to do something when we know that it is wrong? Or why we sometimes say, "We don't know" when we really do?

After this discussion, it may be appropriate to add the following,

Teacher: Sometimes it may be important to consider others when making difficult decisions about telling the truth. For instance, the Geis family, who hid Anne Frank during the Second World War, had to lie in order to keep the Franks safe from harm. Jean Valjean, in a famous story called *Les Miserables*, steals a loaf of bread to feed his starving daughter. And yet, we know it's wrong to lie. We know it's wrong to steal.

When we choose to do what we know to be wrong in order to do what we believe is right, it is important that we know very clearly for ourselves why we are making those decisions.

These are big issues. I wonder if anyone has anything to say? [Students may or may not offer]

Or, move directly to the following,

Teacher: It seems to me that this is a very mature and sophisticated story for a children's picture book. Some people might say that is it not meant for children. What do you think? Why might people say something like that? [They offer]

If you were the librarian for this school, what reasons would you give to your teachers for choosing this book for our library?

We have worked inside this story and explored a story of friendship. Like all friendships, they sometimes can be complicated. Let's hear how the author finishes the story.

Teacher reads from: ***I jump up and run to my bedroom*** … to the end.

Just talk to your neighbours and think about what ways might the author's story connect to the story we have just made together.

Depending upon what the students say, what issues they raise and the level of their understanding, we offer the following questions to help with the discussion.

Teacher: When might we be in a situation where we are asked to stand up for (or protect) our friends?

At the beginning of the story, we identified the differences between Margarita's home and that of Rosario and Chepe. What kinds of effect could that have on their friendship?

OPTION FOR OLDER STUDENTS

If you are working with older students, after completing Activity 10.

11. Dawning consciousness ***As much as needed***

Grouping:	**Whole group**
Strategy:	**Discussion and, if appropriate; improvisation**
Administration:	**Page 21 illustration on an OHP or other media**
Focus:	**To explore the complexities of inequality**

Teacher: Let's revisit the illustration on page 21. What do you see?

In answering this question, students may notice that there is another person helping the children cover the tricycle. If they do not see this, you may need to point it out.

Teacher: To whom might this arm belong? [They suggest]

If that is who you think it might be, what are the implications of this new piece of information? [They discuss]

What now might be the conversation between Juanita and her children?

This is a really difficult scene for the students to improvise unless they have already had some exposure to contemporary issues of social injustices. They may understand the difference between "wants" and "needs", "right" and "wrong"; nevertheless, the complexities of economic inequality may pose deeper challenges. This story drama structure provides a context in which to explore current issues such as the Occupy movement, homelessness and child poverty. See Lundy (2008) for further ideas.

Materials

We assume there is a board and chalk or pens available

Activity 1: Set of keys; blindfold; rolled up newspaper; chairs, jar for names
Activity 2: Whiteboard; pen
Activity 3: Text of *Tricycle*; OHP or other media; illustration of volcano (p. 5)

Activity 5: Text of *Tricycle*
Activity 7: Paper; pencils
Activity 8: Shawl for mother
Activity 9: Large, old cardboard box; shawl for Juanita
Activity 10: Text of *Tricycle*
Activity 11: Illustration on page 21. OHP or other media

Resources

Amado, E. (2007). *Tricycle*. Toronto, ON: Groundwood Books/House of Anansi Press.

Lundy, K. (2008). *Teaching fairly in an unfair world*. Markham, ON: Pembroke Publishers.

Chapter Six

Now, Write!

Based on *The Composition,* written by Antonio Skármeta and illustrated by Alphonso Ruano

Why Did We Choose This Story?

- This is adult-themed story told from the perspective of a child.
- The story personalizes the struggle that all oppressed people experience under a dictatorship.
- By setting the story in another country and another culture, the story provides the distance that allows us examine issues of bullying.
- The story provides an interdisciplinary approach to social studies and the hidden curriculum of ethical behaviour.
- The illustrations provide rich opportunities for interpretation and perspective-taking. There is a great deal of non-verbal text to be read and many spaces for the imagination to roam.
- *The Composition* was the winner of the Américus Book Award and the Jane Adams Award for the best picture book promoting peace and social justice.

Key Understandings and Questions

- There are many ways to use power for control.
- When does it become important to get involved?
- How is it that dictatorships are able to thrive?
- What drives the decision to take a stand?
- What causes someone to remain a bystander?

1. What Pedro wrote — ***4 minutes***

Grouping: **Whole class**

Strategy: **Reading aloud**

Administration: **A copy of Pedro's composition to read; and as an overhead or other media**

Focus: **To enter the story**

Teacher: The story we are going to be working with today takes place many thousands of miles away from where we live and distant from our experiences. Yet it is about things with which we are all familiar. I'd like you to listen carefully to a short excerpt. Its words are the ones out of which we will begin our work.

Teacher reads Pedro's composition on the second last page of the text.

Teacher: Would it be helpful if I read it again?

If yes,

Teacher: If you would like to follow along, I will display it for you to read.

As I do so, think about what you will be listening for as I read these words again.

Some students process information more effectively if they can read the words as they hear them. Teacher reads again.

Teacher: Having heard the composition, the title of our story, we need to take a little time to explore the context (or situation) that would have produced this piece of writing.

2. Seeing the world that Pedro inhabits ***15 minutes***

Grouping: **The size of the groups depends upon the group skills of your students; with senior students use four groups; with younger students use six groups**

Strategy: **Tableaux**

Administration: **One copy of Pedro's composition per group**

Focus: **To see the world that Pedro inhabits**

Teacher: Please get into groups of equal numbers. Group A over here, Group B here and Group C here. Group D here. [If necessary]

If the class is large and you want to have smaller groups, two groups can create tableaux based on the same instruction.

Teacher: Please sit.

105Each group will be creating a tableau based on Pedro's composition. The tasks are going to require you to work with great imagination because you will be using the skills of interpretation.

Each group will present their interpretation through a still picture or tableau. Everyone must be in the tableau and it should incorporate as many ideas as you can. Some of those ideas may seem contradictory. In drama, often that is where we learn the most.

Group A, please stand. From the words of Pedro's composition, what does his writing tell you about his life at home with his family? Using everyone, create a tableau of how his family spends time together.

Group B, please stand. What does Pedro's writing tell you about his school and school culture? What kind of classroom would we see? Using everyone, create a tableau that shows us something about his school life.

Group C, please stand. What does Pedro's composition tell you about the kinds of teachers who would give this assignment? What might we see that would tell us something about them? Using everyone, create a tableau of how we might see these teachers in the staff room. Are they sitting together? Off on their own? What might be the mood of that staff room?

For larger classes, you may include,

Teacher: Group D, please stand. In what kind of a society might Pedro's story take place? What words would you use to describe that society and how would you depict them in a tableau?

We suggest less time in order to promote more focused work. However, as facilitator, you can expand or contract the time, as you move around and check for progress.

Teacher: You have three minutes to generate your ideas and explore them. I will give each group a paper copy of Pedro's composition for reference. [*Hands out papers*]

Try not to spend a lot of time talking. Get up on your feet as soon as you can because that is a good way to stimulate your thinking.

Before moving on to the next strategy, it may be helpful to rehearse the tableaux to make sure that the students are clear about what they are depicting, as the following strategy requires that they hold their ideas while they add to them in another way.

Teacher: Let's just have a little rehearsal. Everyone ready? I am going to count down from three and by the end you should be in your tableau. Hold it for a count of three and, on the last count of three, slowly relax. [They do]

Quickly make any adjustments. [They do]

Are we ready to move on?

3. Building context through words ***15 minutes***

Grouping:	**As above**
Strategy:	**Captioning**
Administration:	**Sentence strips and markers**
Focus:	**To synthesize and concretize ideas in a variety of forms**

Teacher: Before we share our tableaux, there is one more task. I am going to give each group a sentence strip. Now, listen carefully.

Group A: Your task is to write one line of dialogue spoken by someone that will expand our understanding of Pedro's family.

Group B: What is the school motto that hangs in each classroom and over the main entrance to the school? In other words, what is the phrase or sentence that Pedro's school asks its students to remember every day?

Group C: What is the comment that Pedro's teacher writes on his composition that tells us more about the teacher?

If you have a fourth group,

Teacher: Group D: Write no more than four adjectives that might describe the society in which Pedro lives.

Students compose. The time needed depends on the group.

Teacher: Are we ready to share? [They agree]

We will begin by seeing the group A's interpretation of Pedro's family life. As the groups are getting ready here [*indicates space*], the rest of you close your eyes. I will count down from five and say, "open". We will look at each tableaux and I will read the caption. In this way, we can expand our understanding of Pedro's life.

This is very challenging because the presenters need to hold still while we take in all the information they will be giving us.

See and hear each tableau in this way and when all have been presented,

Teacher: In your own group, talk together about what you have seen. [They do]

Those were really powerful images and have given a lot to think about. What new ideas and understandings would you like to share with us all? [They share]

We are beginning to get an idea of Pedro's world. Pedro's world doesn't seem to be that much different from our own.

Depending on the time, this could be the conclusion of your lesson. If not,

Teacher: Let's see what else we can discover.

4. Meeting Pedro ***5 minutes***

Grouping: **Whole class**
Strategy: **Reading a picture**
Administration: **Picture of Pedro at the wall; OHP & screen or other projection media**
Focus: **To explore the picture**

Teacher: Sit down where you can see the picture. Just as you listened so carefully before, now look very carefully at a picture from our story.

What do we see/notice?

Where do we see it?

What is the focus of the picture?

What do you see in this picture that might tell us something about the story we are about to enter?

This last question can act as a bridge to the next set of questions that explore subtext (reading as an author).

Teacher: What might be the mood of this picture?

What other things might be going on?

What might this person be thinking?

What leads you to say that?

What might this story be about? [They contribute]

Thank you. You've created a very rich background for this story.

5. Thinking as authors and illustrators ***20 minutes***

Grouping: **Class divided into six new groups**

Strategy: **Story mapping and matching text**

Administration: **Set of seven pictures from text; six excerpts from the text**

Focus: **To enhance students' interpretative abilities by enabling them to visualize story characters, events and settings**

Teacher: In your groups, number yourselves from 1 to 4 (or 5, depending on class size). Ones, in this corner, twos in that corner, etc. [They move to places indicated]

Now that we are in new groups, we have a new task.

I am giving each group a set of pictures from our story. Thinking as illustrators, your first task is to put the pictures in order as you imagine the story. This is harder than it seems. You probably won't arrive at a version that suits everyone but work for consensus. You have about five minutes.

After about five or so minutes,

Teacher: Stop what you are doing. Now, here is the challenge.

Each group will receive a set of six excerpts from the text.

This time, thinking as authors, decide which piece of text belongs to which picture. There will be one picture with no text. [They sort]

Depending upon how you have laid out the illustrations, write one sentence that helps us to understand the picture without text and its place in the story. You may need to shift some of the pictures. We are looking for meaning.

As teacher walks around the groups, it will become clear when it is time to move on. There will be some groups that don't complete the task. This is not a problem because they are in a process of interpretation.

Teacher: Let's move around the room and see what each group has created. You may notice some inconsistencies. Don't judge which version is correct because they all reflect the group's authorship. Talk to each other about what you see and where you agree and how your ideas change as you view these different versions.

Groups move clockwise around the room seeing how others interpreted the story.

Teacher: Go back to your own story version and talk together about the other versions you have just seen. [They do]

In sequencing the story, what were your challenges?

Think back to the picture of the boy and the wall. How close was your initial reading of the image of the boy now that you have more of the story?

In drama, it is important to connect the fiction to students' own experiences. That's where understanding and deeper learning occur.

What knowledge or experiences led you to the assumptions you made as you put text to picture? [They talk together and if appropriate, share]

6. To whom should we talk? ***10 minutes***

Grouping: **As above**

Strategy: **Preparing for hot-seating**

Administration: **Paper and pencil for each group**

Focus: **To decide who is best equipped to help us in our drama; to generate questions that will move us forward**

Teacher: In your groups think about the illustrations and predictions you have made. Decide on the person we need to meet in order to know more about the story. Who has the potential to offer us the kind of information that will move our drama into the heart of the story? To whom can we talk?

Once you have decided on that person, create four questions that you need to ask that person and record them. I'll give you paper and pencil. You have four minutes.

Teacher distributes paper and pencils.

Teacher: Let's hear from each group whom they have chosen and the questions they would ask of that person. [They share]

Now that we've heard from each group, let's decide together which one of those choices might provide the greatest dramatic potential for deepening our work. [Students suggest. For example, they decide they want to hear from the Teacher in the story]

Would you be willing to accept me in role as the Teacher?

By hearing the suggestions of the groups, the teacher has had an opportunity to prepare for the role upon which the class decides. The following offers a way to begin and provides an example of the teacher in role as Pedro's Teacher.

7. Hearing from a character in the story — ***5 minutes***

Grouping: **Whole class**

Strategy: **Teacher in role; hot seating**

Administration: **Chair for the teacher in role; article or piece of clothing as signifier**

Focus: **To fold new information into old; to encourage focused listening**

Once the teacher knows which role to undertake, only the attitudes and points of view are necessary, although it is sometimes helpful to have something to indicate the role; for example, an apron for the mother, a pile of papers for the teacher, and so on.

Teacher enters in role and sits in chair:

I know I've kept you waiting a long time. Thank you for your patience. What is it that you would like to know? Who has the first question?

This activity does not have to go on for long, just enough for the students to gain something that might help them to develop the drama. The teacher's task is to offer responses that are true to the role. How the teacher responds can offer a new or different perspective. For example:

Student: How do you feel about a person from the military coming in to your classroom?

Teacher in role as The Teacher: I have no choice. The principal informed me and must agree. I need the money. I am the only support in the family.

When questions cease to move things forward, teacher says,

Teacher: Thank you for your interest in my life. I rarely get to talk to people like yourselves on a one-to-one basis. However, I have another appointment (other duties) that I must attend to.

Teacher rises and moves to another space, signifying that she is now out of role.

Teacher: Well. Those were some wonderful questions.

What do we know now that we didn't before? [They share]

What was it that you heard that surprised you? [They share]

Let's keep those ideas in mind as we hear the author's version of the story.

8. Pedro's story — ***5 minutes***

Grouping:	**Whole class**
Strategy:	**Reading aloud**
Administration:	**Text of *The Composition***
Focus:	**To hear the story against the background of students' own versions**

Teacher reads the whole story and shows the pictures as the story is read.

Teacher: Talk to the person next to you about this story and how it matches or is different from your interpretations.

What was it, I wonder, that made Pedro realize the kind of composition he needed to write? Let's hear your ideas. [They share]

9. What is Pedro thinking about? — ***3 minutes***

Grouping:	**Whole class divided into two rows; a volunteer to be Pedro**
Strategy:	**Conscience alley**
Administration:	**Perhaps a schoolbag for Pedro to carry**
Focus:	**To explore decision-making**

Teacher: Who will volunteer to take on the role of Pedro? You don't have to speak but to listen very hard to what is being said as you move slowly down the line. [Student volunteers]

The rest of you will make two lines, leaving enough room for Pedro to walk between them. [They do]

As Pedro moves slowly down the alley you make for him, we will hear the thoughts that are going through his mind as he left school on the day of the Captain's visit.

Be aware that only one person will speak at a time so that Pedro can hear what you have to say.

Any questions?

Sometimes students are a little confused, especially if they have not worked with this strategy before. Clear up the difficulties before you begin so that the power of the feelings is not interrupted.

Teacher: Perhaps it would help us to make it more real if Pedro carries his book bag.

What do you think?

If they agree, teacher gives the bag to the volunteer.

Teacher: Are there any questions before we begin? Remember, Pedro, walk slowly enough so that you hear every thought.

If there are any problems as the strategy moves along, stop it quietly and sort it out. Then ask the student in role as Pedro to begin again

Teacher: Thank you. Hearing those words in your head, find your own space. Sit down.

10. Pedro's advice to his son ***As long as needed***

Grouping: **Individual**
Strategy: **Writing in role**
Administration: **Paper and pencil for each student; box for letters**
Focus: **To describe a time in history**

Teacher: I'd like you to imagine that you are Pedro, now a father. It is 30 years since you wrote that composition when you were ten. Now, you have a son the same age as you were at that time. Tomorrow is his tenth birthday. What would you say to him in your letter to mark that occasion? As his father, what part of your family history do you need to share with him? What will you say to him about that time, when you were a schoolboy 30 years ago? [They write]

Be sure to give students enough time and don't worry if they stop writing for a while. In our experience they are thinking hard.

Teacher: It is time to finish. What will you say in closing and how will you sign your letter? Remember you are now an adult with a little boy of your own.

Read over what you have written. Take a moment to add anything or make any changes. When you are ready, fold up your letter and put a mark on the outside that only you will recognize. This will prevent you from working with your own letter. [They do]

Bring it to the centre of the room and put it in this box over here. [They do]

Teacher: I am going to give each of you a letter from Pedro's father.

Teacher gives each student a letter to read as s/he says,

Teacher: Please don't open your letter yet because you need to do something very important. I am going to ask you to switch roles so that when you read the letter, you are to read it in role as Pedro's ten-year-old son. This is what your father needs to say to you on the occasion of your tenth birthday. You may open your letter now. [They begin reading]

Out of role now. What sentences made this letter come alive for you? Let's hear some of those things that Pedro wants his son to know. [They share around]

OPTION

This option offers students the opportunity to reconsider how their initial assumptions of the story may have changed. Teacher may want to remind students of their initial tasks. Refer to instructions for Activities 2 and 3 for sharing tableaux and captions.

Teacher: We now have an opportunity to revisit the first activity we did to set up the context of the story. Please get back into your original groups, As, Bs, Cs (and Ds). Knowing what you now know, re-create the tableaux in light of all the new understandings you have gained. You may want, as well, to change the caption.

11. Reflection ***As needed***

Grouping:	**Whole class**
Strategy:	**Discussion**
Administration:	**None**
Focus:	**To generate thinking beyond the story**

Teacher: There are many examples of power in this story. Talk to the person next to you about what some of those might be. How is that power demonstrated?

What are the risks of standing up for your family or a friend, as Pedro did?

I wonder whether there was ever a time in your life or the life of someone we may know when you or they were faced with a difficult choice?

I wonder what might be some of the conditions that would allow a dictatorship to take over a country? I wonder if it could happen here?

Extensions

Game: Augusto Boal's game of "Enemy and Protector".

Improvisation: What was life like for the parents of the boy before he was born and what dreams did they have for their son? Improvise a conversation that would allow us to learn about their expectations for their son?

Writing: The composition that won the captain's prize.

Presentation: Our colleague, Darcy McNee, describes how she and her grade eight students concluded the story drama structure.

"I had the students write a composition in role as students in Pedro's class. On the day they were to present, I put the motto that one of the groups had come up with earlier, on the board. I copied the picture from p. 25 of Captain Romero, cut out the background—then placed it in a frame and hung it in the classroom. The students stood and said the motto in unison while looking at the captain's picture. Each student then presented his/her composition. I set up a video camera and taped each student, telling them that the tape would be sent to the Leader for the competition". (Email, March 20, 2012)

Role on the wall: What adjectives would you use to describe Pedro?

Storytelling:	After students hear the story, in groups of up to six, they retell the story from the points of view of the characters in the story, switching every few sentences: Pedro; Daniel, the grocer; Pedro's teacher; Pedro's mother; Pedro's father; the captain.
Research:	What happened in Chile at the time of the story? How has that country changed? What other countries do we know of where the struggle for democracy still exists?

Materials

Activity 1: A copy of Pedro's composition to read and as an overhead or other media
Activity 2: One copy of the composition per group
Activity 3: Sentence strips and markers
Activity 4: Illustration of Pedro at the wall, OHP & screen or other media
Activity 5: Set of seven pictures from text:

1. p. 2: Pedro with ball, parents seated behind.
2. p. 7: Daniel's father being arrested.
3. p. 10: Daniel with the keys.
4. p. 18: Captain Romero, the teacher and children standing.
5. p. 20: The eraser, pencil and paper
6. p. 22: Pedro and Juan side by side
7. p. 25: The captain in profile

Six excerpts from the text (see Figure 2)
Activity 6: Paper and pencil for each group
Activity 7: Chair for the teacher in role; article or piece of clothing as signifier
Activity 8: Text of *The Composition*
Activity 9: School bag
Activity 10: Paper and pencil for each student; box for letters

Resources

Boal, A. (1992). *Games for actors and non-actors* (A. Jackson, Trans.). London: Routledge.

Skármeta, A. (2000). *The composition* (E. Amado, Trans.). Toronto: Groundwood Books.

"What does it say?"
"Things about us, about our country."
"How come it's so hard to hear?" he demanded.
"The voices are a long way away," his mother answered.

Up and down the street, windows were opening. People were craning around the corner to see. Some doors slammed shut.

"They arrest people for that?" asked Pedro.
"I think so," answered Daniel.
"What are you going to do?" asked Pedro.
"I don't know," said Daniel.

"I am Captain Romero and I'm here on behalf of the government, that is to say, General Perdomo, to invite the children in this school to write a composition."

"Take out your notebooks. Notebooks at the ready? Take out your pencils. Pencils at the ready? Write! Title of the composition? What my family does at night."

"My dear young friends," he said, "your compositions were very nice and made us soldiers very happy."

Figure 2: Text excerpts for Activity 5. May be photocopied for classroom use. © 2016 *Into the Story 2: More Stories! More Drama!* by Carole Miller and Juliana Saxton. Bristol, UK: Intellect.

Chapter Seven

The Wealth of the Sea

Based on *The Fish Princess,* written by Irene Watts and illustrated by Steve Mennie

Why Did We Choose This Story?

- In almost every culture, there are many stories—fables, fairy and folk tales, myths—that are told about the sea and those who come from it to live on the land.
- *The Fish Princess* embodies universal themes of love, exclusion and sacrifice. It holds implications for how we use our natural resources.
- The illustrations are infused with the sense of a distant time and place, evoking the mood underlying the story and providing rich extensions for the narrative.
- We all share an innate resistance to difference. This story acts as a powerful metaphor that helps us to understand the place of "other" that exists in each of us.

Key Understandings and Questions

- Old stories that involve the mysteries of the sea were told for a reason.
- What is it about a stranger that causes us to turn away?
- How does the love of another manifest itself in sacrifice?
- To what degree are we each other's other?
- What is it that motivates the human desire for excess?

<u>*1. Exploring the words*</u> **<u>*10 minutes*</u>**

Grouping:	**Four (or five) groups of equal or near equal size**
Strategy:	**Brainstorming**
Administration:	**Large chart paper (one for each group) with single word written in large capitals in the middle of the page; coloured felt pens**
Focus:	**To build collaborative meanings**

Divide class into four or five groups. Each group is given a large sheet of paper and a number of felt pens. Each sheet has one of the following words written on it:

Group	**Words**
A	ABUNDANCE
B	GREED
C	INCLUSION
D	SHUNNING
E	LOVE (if needed)

If you feel your class works best in smaller groups, more than one group may interpret the same word.

<u>Teacher:</u> Each group, please gather around one of these pieces of paper. Here we have Group A, Group B, Group C and Group D (etc.) [They arrange themselves]

Using the coloured pens that you find by each paper, write your response to the word in the centre of the page. You may respond with one word, with a short phrase or, if you feel an image would be more useful, draw your response. Because we are brainstorming, you may build on each other's ideas. Generate as many responses as you can in the short time you have. These responses are going to be an important resource for our later work.

Ready? Off you go.

There may be some talking and the short time frame means that there is a lot of space left on the page. After two minutes or so,

Teacher: In a moment, I am going to ask you to move on to where the group next to you has been working. So think about finishing up.

Right. Put down your pens. Group A, move along to Group B's paper; Group B to Group C's and Group C move on to Group D's and Group D to Group A's. [They do]

Take a moment to read the responses and when you are ready to add your own words, use any of the pens available. Remember, you can write wherever you wish, this does not have to be linear.

Allow students to take the time to read what has been written before they start adding. Again, after not more than two to three minutes,

Teacher: Right, everyone put down your pens and move along to the next paper. Take your time to read the responses and then add your own. [They do]

When all the groups are one stage away from their starting point,

Teacher: And, last change. I know that these pages are filling up but find the room you need to add your thoughts to these collective responses.

When students have added their own responses,

Teacher: Good. Now each group return to your original paper and take the time to read everything that has been written and added to your original ideas. As you do this, talk together about what you are reading; what surprises you; what new ideas have been added? [They do]

2. Words into images *20 minutes*

Grouping:	**Groups as above**
Strategy:	**Tableau**
Administration:	**Each group's word response page; a working space for each group**
Focus:	**Translating collective response into a physical representation**

Teacher: Our task now is for each group to take what is written on your paper and translate those ideas into a three-dimensional visual image, a tableau. Take the essence of what is on your page and what you have talked about and find a way to portray your collective response to those ideas.

When we have created our tableaux we will have four still images that represent our collective responses to each word. We will have an opportunity to read these tableaux, so pay attention to every sign that you are making with your bodies: consider expression, gesture and shape. Be sure that your focus is clear.

This is not an easy task and so we need to have a bit of time. How much time do you think you will need?

It is a good idea to give students an opportunity to direct their own work process. Sometimes they will give themselves too long. If they ask for five minutes, suggest that you will announce when three minutes are up, so they can see how much more time they will need. Sometimes they give themselves too little time. In that case, tell them when their time is up and suggest another minute or two. It is always better to work with less time rather than more.

Teacher can move from group to group and act as an outside eye when the group is almost ready to present. You might say, "This is what I see" *so that the group can make adjustments to clarify the points they need to make. When they appear to have finished,*

Teacher: Right. We have some wonderfully interesting tableaux to read.

I wonder, if before we share them, you could think of a title that might be appropriate for your tableaux. Don't write anything down, just have it in your heads. [They take a minute to discuss and decide]

This synthesizing technique is a useful means of helping each group listen, as they are frozen, to what their audience is saying in response to their work.

Teacher: Who would like to go first? This is going to take a lot of focus and concentration both for the presenters and for the observers.

Groups may want to order themselves or go at random.

Teacher: I will ask everyone watching to close their eyes as the group gets into position. [Group makes tableau, watchers close eyes]

Open.

Let them look for a moment without saying anything, then,

Teacher: This tableau is responding to the word "__________".

After a moment to put the word to the picture, use any one or more of the following questions to generate responses for collective understanding:

- What do we see here?
- What sorts of actions do you see?
- What mood is being represented?
- What kinds of feelings are expressed in the tableau?
- What sorts of feelings does the tableau generate in you?

As the groups share their work, you may add in different questions or suggestions. After all tableaux have been shared,

Teacher:	Before we move into our story, I expect that each group would like to have an opportunity to talk together about their responses to what they heard. [They do]

Reflection is very important. Try and keep the process moving along and be aware of the pace and the flow of ideas.

3. How it all began ***2 minutes***

Grouping:	**Whole class**
Strategy:	**Narration**
Administration:	**None**
Focus:	**To introduce the form and context for the story**

Teacher: Find somewhere comfortable for a moment while you listen as we introduce the story. [They do]

In almost every culture, there are many stories—fables, fairy and folk tales, myths—that are told about the sea and those who come from it to live on the land. Old stories like that were told for a reason. Our story is drawn from a number of these tales and our work will be to discover what meanings it may hold for us today.

This story takes place a long time ago in a fishing village somewhere on a rocky coast. For some of us, that is a familiar landscape, but for others, it is not in their experience. This is a land where the coastline is rocky. This is a place where the wind howls against the cliffs. This is a sea that feeds and sustains our people, but it is also a sea that can turn angry.

I wonder what words or phrases we could use that would help us all to understand that environment? We need to think about not only what would be seen but also what we might hear and feel and taste, as well. [They offer]

It may be enough to hear the words and phrases or it might be useful to list them.

Teacher: Thank you, those words will be useful to us in our next bit of work.

4. Becoming the sea and the shore ***10 minutes***

Grouping: **Whole class, numbered off as one or two**

Strategy: **Movement**

Administration: **Sea music (suggest: Debussy's *La Mer*; Mendelssohn's *Fingals Cave Overture*); tambourine**

Focus: **To create a sense of the sea**

Teacher: Spread into space with even distances between you. In a moment, as you move around, keep that same distance between each other. As you move, think about the water and how it shapes and dissolves. Think about the rocks and their shapes and the fact that they never move at all but always see what is happening. Let the music guide you. [They do]

Let them move for about a minute or until you see that they are getting the flow and then use the tambourine as a signal or just lower the music.

Now, I'd like you to think about the shore: the smooth stones, the jagged rocks, or something that the sea has thrown up onto the beach. Choose one of those objects. Now explore that shape: the roundness of the smooth stones, the angles of the jagged rocks, the nooks and crannies of the seaweeds, shells and driftwood. I'll put the music on for you to try out some ideas. Remember to consider your size, your shape, height and levels and remember to keep your spaces. [They do]

Let them explore and when the shaping of their bodies is becoming clear,

Teacher (*over the music*): When you hear the tambourine, freeze into that object that you have been exploring, so that we can see the shape of the coastline.

After a moment, sound the tambourine.

Teacher: Good! There were some lovely and interesting shapes being explored. Now, let's put this seascape together.

Turn to the person next to you and decide who is number one and who is number two. Equal numbers are not that important. [They do]

Everyone, once again, spread into the space, equal distances. And we will all begin flowing through the room as the water. When you hear the music, allow it to guide your movement, your pace. Continue to maintain the spaces between each other.

Allow for a minute or so of movement and then teacher sounds the tambourine and says, over the music,

Teacher: Ones: Freeze into a new shape that represents your part of the shore.

Twos: continue to move as waves in and out of the shoreline and through the spaces and crevices surrounding you. Each time you hear the tambourine, if you feel ready, change from sea to shore and feel the waves washing over and around you; or shore to sea and feel yourself flowing around and through.

Continue for a minute or so. If they are ready to change on their own, let them change to their own timing.

Teacher: And stop. Just turn to the person next to you and talk together about that experience. [They do]

What challenged you? What did you notice? What moods were occurring? What connections were you making with one another? [They talk]

Does anyone have anything to share?

This is an opportunity to acknowledge how movement can be used to express context and provides an atmosphere that they can draw on for the work to come.

Teacher: Thank you. Remember all those thoughts as we move into our story.

5. The arrival of the child ***3 minutes***

Grouping: **Whole class**
Strategy: **Story reading**
Administration: **Text of *The Fish Princess***
Focus: **To introduce the protagonist**

Teacher: Just rest where you are and listen.

Teacher reads from: ***Before she learned to speak, she sang songs of the wind-whipped waves*** … to … ***no one knew from where she had come or to whom she belonged.***

6. Why should we be afraid? *10 minutes*

Grouping:	**Whole class**
Strategy:	**Gossip mill**
Administration:	**5 x 3 cards, pencils for each person; tambourine**
Focus:	**To develop the attitude of the villagers towards the baby**

Teacher: I wonder what we have heard in our story so far that would cause the villagers to be afraid? Think about that. What sorts of things might cause them to become fearful? Would it help if I read you that again?

Reading the excerpt again allows students to listen in another way.

Teacher: Just talk with the person next to you and share your ideas of what would make these adult villagers afraid of a child? [They do]

Give them only a minute to share. This is really a technique to generate ideas and to give courage to those who have already something in mind. You may want to hear some suggestions before,

Teacher: Come and take a card and a pencil and find yourself a quiet space. Imagine that you are one of the villagers. Write down two or three phrases or sentences that express your fears about this new child. They might express something very deep that you could only whisper or they might express something you would be happy to say aloud.

Give a couple of minutes for this.

Teacher: Good. Now, pick up your card and read those words over to yourself. Note which you would be prepared to say aloud and those that you would be too afraid (for whatever reason) to do more than whisper to a close friend.

Mark with a "W", anything that you would only be prepared to whisper. Mark with an "A", anything that you would be prepared to say aloud. [They do]

Take a moment to commit those words to memory.

From where you are, let's try those out—whispering and speaking aloud, as if you were talking to yourself—all together and all at once. It will be noisy but that's OK. We're rehearsing.

Sometimes it is a good idea to rattle the tambourine; this covering sound allows them to experiment with more confidence.

Teacher: Good. Put your card and pencil away some place where you can find them easily and quickly.

Note: These cards will be needed for Activity 10.

Teacher: Gather into the centre of the room.

Close your eyes and think of what has happened: the arrival of the baby; what the sea has thrown up and of what that may mean for the village and for you as a member of that community.

In a moment, we are going to create a scene of the members of this community sharing their fears and by doing so, bonding together against those fears.

When you hear the word, "Begin", move around amongst each other, speaking of those things that you fear. Use your own stage directions either to whisper or to say aloud. You have two or three phrases or sentences, try them out and see which one or ones really work for you and for the scene. When you hear the tambourine, freeze. [They do]

Give about 30 seconds to try things out, just enough time for the students to get the hang of it. After the tambourine,

Teacher: What were some things you heard that really caught the mood of fear? [They share]

Let's try that again and now that we know the potential for this scene, see if we can find a way to build it. When it feels right, see if we can find a way to finish it that is both true to the mood we are creating and also theatrically satisfying.

Students may want to try this a number of times until they find a rhythm and pace that works for them.

Teacher: Now we have created the setting and know something about the people in this community. Let us now look at our protagonists.

7. Who cares for her? ***1 minute***

Grouping: **Whole class**
Strategy: **Story reading**
Administration: **Text of *The Fish Princess***
Focus: **To introduce the fisherman**

Teacher: Just stay where you are and listen.

Teacher reads from: ***The villagers feared the child for she was not of their kind*** … to … ***She was his only family, and he was hers.***

8. Meeting the fisherman ***7 minutes***

Grouping: **Whole class**
Strategy: **Teacher in role**
Administration: **Old shirt; net for mending; chair in centre**
Focus: **To discover what kind of man would stand against his village**

Teacher: I wonder what kind of person you would have to be in those days of suspicion and superstition, to stand against your community?

Teacher puts chair with shirt and net in the middle of the room.

Teacher: The next work we're going to do is challenging. It requires us to listen hard and to keep the dialogue as real as we can.

Come and gather around this chair. Leave enough space so that we are not crowding the chair and its props. We need to leave room for our imaginations.

The chair and its props represent the fisherman. Our job is to find out what sort of man this is, a man who would go against the world of the village, a man who would go against the gods that look after them.

I wonder what sorts of things we might say to him? What sorts of questions might we ask him that would help us to understand him? Anyone have a suggestion? [They suggest]

Hear only a few, just enough to prime the pump, then,

Teacher: And I wonder what sorts of answers he might give? Anyone?

Again, hear a few. This is a rehearsal for the next step in the activity. Hearing these questions and answers allows the teacher to have some ideas about what might be asked and how it could be answered.

Teacher: Good. Now, let's see how we can make this work. Would you be willing to accept me as the fisherman? When I put on this shirt, it will be a reminder that we are talking to the child's grandfather. Remember, our task is to discover what makes this man different from the rest of the community. Who will ask the first question?

Establish this before going into role.

Teacher: Are we ready to meet the grandfather?

Teacher puts on the shirt and sits on the chair. S/he may choose to pick up the net; working on it can provide opportunities to pause and think about an answer.

Teacher in role: These storms have played havoc with my nets. Good to see you all. Nice to have an opportunity to talk.

Let the dialogue go on for a few minutes. You may want to stop after a few exchanges and check that everyone is clear as to what is happening. You may want to reiterate the purpose by asking, "So, what kind of a man is beginning to emerge from our conversation?" *Or it may move forward on its own without your intervention. When ready, conclude with,*

Teacher in role: We should take more time to meet with one another but fishing is fishing and we all need to get back to work.

Teacher gets up, taking off shirt and role,

Teacher: Just turn to the person next to you and talk together about what we have discovered about the fisherman. [They do]

Who has something they would like to share? [They share]

If appropriate, the teacher might wish to comment on the fact that it is not too surprising that people might be wary about the child.

9. Life passes **_1 minute_**

Group:	**Whole class**
Strategy:	**Story reading**
Administration:	**Text of *The Fish Princess***
Focus:	**To learn how they lived their lives**

Teacher: Just listen to the next bit of our story.

Teacher reads from: ***The villagers shunned the fisherman and the girl*** … to … ***she sat apart.***

10. The daily round **_10 minutes_**

Grouping:	**Pairs**
Strategy:	**Improvisation**
Administration:	**5 x 3 cards and pencils from Activity 6**
Focus:	**To examine the relationship between the two**

Teacher: In a moment, we are going to improvise some brief scenes that will give us a picture of the everyday lives of these two people.

Find a partner and decide who is to be the fisherman and who will be the girl. [They do]

Decide what part of the day your scene will take place—morning, afternoon or evening. [They do]

Decide where it will take place. [They do]

Decide what they are doing together. [They do]

The focus of these brief improvisations is to not only tell us what it is the girl and her grandfather do during the day, but, equally important, your scene will tell us something about how they get on together, about their relationship.

Decide with your partner what the scene might be about. You should have a number of ideas so that you can choose what will work best in your opinion, to help us understand their relationship.

Let them work it out for three to four minutes while teacher circulates to check for understanding and to provide guidance.

Teacher: There are some really interesting ideas at work here. Please go and get your cards and your pencils. For this first part, we will work individually.

We are now working as playwrights. Turn your card over and remembering your improvisation, write the line or lines of dialogue that you feel best tells us about your relationship. For example, if you played the Child you might have said something like, "It's lunchtime, grandpa, what would you like to eat?" or, as Grandpa: "Your little fingers are quite raw from mending the nets." [They do]

Share what you each have written. Your task is to expand the two lines of dialogue that you have into a four-line scene. Of course, you may want to expand or change some words. What is important is how you will show us that relationship in a short scene that will help us to know these two people better. How can you show us what they are doing in this scene? [They work it out]

You may want to do a rehearsal, that is, everyone working at the same time. This technique helps to focus the work and gives students an opportunity to refine.

Teacher:	We are ready to share these scenes now. How shall we arrange to see them? [They suggest] We will see these scenes in that order, as if we were looking at short film clips. We won't stop to reflect until we have seen them all. Arrange yourselves so that we can all see each other. [They do] Ready? Begin.

After they have all shared,

Teacher:	Just sit down and talk to your partner about what you now know. [They do] Is there any scene that you would like to see again? [They say]

Often, there will be one or two scenes that need repeating. Ask the group to reset themselves and repeat. Allow for pair reflections on that (or those).

Teacher:	Thank you. What do we know now about this relationship that we did not know before? [They share]

11. The wealth of the sea ***1 minute***

Grouping:	**Whole class**
Strategy:	**Teacher narration**
Administration:	**Adapted text**
Focus:	**Setting up the climax of the story**

Teacher narrates:	The years passed. And each year, the salmon returned. No one went hungry and all became accustomed to the wealth of the sea. No one thought

to associate the baby's arrival with this abundance, neither the villagers nor the fisherman himself. No one spoke of it at all and neither did the child.

On the 16th anniversary of her arrival, the girl (for such she was now) and the fisherman went out to fish as usual. They took from the sea, as they always had, only what they could eat and only as much as they could preserve for the coming winter.

When they returned along the shore, they passed, as usual, the villagers bringing in their nets. But this time it was different; the fish were piled even higher, their scales gleaming in the setting sun. Too many to eat, too many to smoke, too many to store. Yet the fishermen continued to slash and gut, slash and gut. Their knives gleamed as they struck again and again. (Adapted from Watts, 1996)

12. The plunder of the sea — ***5 minutes***

Grouping: **Whole class**
Strategy: **Movement**
Administration: **The net; tambourine**
Focus: **To set up the mystery**

Teacher: I am going to lay this net out here.

The net is stretched out on the floor in the middle of the room.

When each of you feels ready, come and take your place around it. [They do]

Take a few moments to practice how you would reach out and take a fish; how you would slash it and gut it; where you would throw it. Remember the faster you work, the greater the haul. You are professionals and those fish are heavy and slippery. Clean them well for they are your livelihood. Listen for the tambourine. It will tell you when to begin and when to stop.
[They do]

Freeze. Remember your position. Relax and listen.

This next time, see if you can use your body more. Make it all bigger: the bending, the slashing, the gutting, the throwing. [They repeat with tambourine signal]

And freeze. Well done.

This time, as you keep on working, see what you would or could add, verbally or non-verbally, to make the scene reflect the words of the story: ***Too many to eat, to smoke, to store. Yet still the knives gleamed as the fishermen struck and struck again.*** [They repeat with tambourine signal]

And freeze. Remember your positions. Remember your words.

This third time should have created a movement piece of some power and urgency.

Teacher: I wonder who has seen or experienced that same kind of intensity, the same kind of feeling that was generated by the scene we have just created? [They offer]

Thank you. What we have just created will serve as a powerful context for our next scene.

13. The heart of the story ***As long as needed***

Grouping: **Whole class**

Strategy: **Casting**

Administration: **Adapted text printed out on a large card (see Figure 3)**

Focus: **To listen**

Teacher: Is there someone who is prepared to read the next fragment of the story? [A volunteer steps forward]

As you hear the words being read, listen very carefully.

Student reads: There was only one great fish remaining. The last of the sun showed the beauty of the colour of its scales as it threw itself against the net. The villager raised his arm, the knife red with blood in the fading light. The girl stepped forward and ***stood beside him, trembling. She stared at the silver blade poised high. Slowly, slowly the knife was lowered—put aside.***

Teacher: Thank you. So who besides the villagers are in this scene? [They identify]

Is there someone who is willing to take on the role of the grandfather? [A volunteer]

Is there someone who will take on the role of the granddaughter? [A volunteer]

Who is willing to become the villager with the knife in this scene? [A volunteer]

Where will these three be positioned in relation to the villagers and their work? [They decide and place]

Good! Let's now see those three people as part of that last frozen image of all of the villagers harvesting the fish. Villagers, take your places. [They re-create as a tableau]

Super! Remember where each one of you is positioned for this scene.

<u>14. How will the story end?</u> ***<u>As long as needed</u>***

Grouping: **Groups of five or six**

Strategy: **Creating the ending**

Administration: **A piece of shiny, glittery fabric to represent the scales of the fish, one for each group; instructions to students projected or printed for each group (see Figure 4)**

Focus: **To interpret a text theatrically**

<u>Teacher:</u> Please get into groups of five (six) now. [They do]
The only piece of information that you now need is the last line of the story, ***And the three turned and walked towards the sea.***

In your groups, you need to think about the kind of story we are working with. It is a fairly tale or myth and those kinds of stories always have a sense of magic, the possibility of transformation. Bearing that in mind, your task is to work out the end of the story, considering all the imaginative possibilities.

* Here is your task. In your groups, you are to cast the scene: characters you have to work with are the grandfather, the girl, the villager with the knife and others, as needed. We know the end of the story: ***And the three turned and walked towards the sea.*** Who those three are is up to you; what happens between the dropping of the knife and ***walking towards the sea*** is up

to you. What you work out will be the way in which you want the story to end.

Decide if you will use dialogue or whether it can be done without words.

Your scene will begin with these lines: ***The girl stepped forward. The arm that was raised hesitated. Slowly the villager lowered his arm and the knife fell from his hand.*** The scene ends with the action, ***And the three turned and walked towards the sea.***

I am going to give each group a piece of fabric that may help you with your decisions.

Let's start with five minutes to plan this out and then we will see if we need more time. Off you go. [They begin]

* *You may want to print out these instructions for each group or project them on some other media. How long they work depends upon their interest, engagement and the quality of work you are seeking.*

15. Presenting interpretations — ***As long as needed***

Grouping:	**Groups of five or six**
Strategy:	**Presentation**
Administration:	**A piece of shiny, glittery fabric to represent the scales of the fish, one for each group; the net**
Focus:	**To discover the imaginative possibilities of interpretation**

When each group has their final scene ready to present, set up the scene around the net to represent the playing space and invite each group to share. After each group has shared and responses generated, the class might like to choose one of the scenes and put the whole ending together, beginning with the movement piece of Activity 12. What bits of text will be used and how this is accomplished is up to the teacher and the group.

16. Reflection ***As long as needed***

Grouping:	**Whole group**
Strategy:	**Reflection**
Administration:	**None**
Focus:	**To relate the drama experience to students' lives**

Some suggested questions:

Take a moment to consider the variety of endings we have just seen. What is it about stories like this that make it possible to create so many versions?

In this story, people were fearful of someone who was different. I wonder why this child caused such fear? Where does that come from?

What other stories do we know where someone was judged unfairly? Where in our lives may we be witness to judgmental attitudes?

What meanings does this story hold for us today?

In this story, abundance was taken for granted, causing even greater need and greed. Our society is considered "rich" in assets. Why then, are we so concerned with the environment?

At this point, you may want to ask the students if they want to hear the end of the story as written by Irene Watts. If so,

Teacher reads from: ***The girl stood beside him, trembling*** … to the end of the story.

What differences did you notice?

Often films that are made from books are different. Why might that be so?

I am thinking of *The Hunger Games* as a model and wondering if this story could be adapted for film?

Materials

Activity 1: Chart paper; felt pens
Activity 2: Completed chart paper
Activity 4: Tambourine; sea music
Activity 5: Text of *The Fish Princess*
Activity 6: 5 x 3 cards; pencils; tambourine
Activity 7: Text of *The Fish Princess*
Activity 8: Old shirt; net; chair
Activity 9: Text of *The Fish Princess*
Activity 10: 5 x 3 cards and pencils from Activity 6
Activity 11: Adapted text
Activity 12: Net, tambourine
Activity 13: Adapted text (see Figure 3)
Activity 14: Five or six pieces of shiny fabric; instructions for groups (see Figure 4)
Activity 15: Fabric; net

Resource

Watts, I. (1996). *The fish princess.* Toronto, ON: Tundra Books.

Additional resources

Booth, D. (2014). *Exploding the reading: Building a world of responses from one story.* Markham, ON: Pembroke Publishers.

Cooper, S. (1991). *The selkie girl.* New York, NY: Aladdin Books.

Mitchell, A. (1996). *Maudie and the green children.* Surrey, England & Vancouver, B.C.: Tradewind Books.

Yagawa, S., & Patterson, K. (Trans.) (1981). *The crane wife.* New York, NY: William Morrow and Company.

There was only one great fish remaining. The last of the sun showed the beauty of the colour of its scales as it threw itself against the net. The villager raised his arm, the knife red with blood in the fading light. The girl stepped forward and ***stood beside him, trembling. She stared at the silver blade poised high. Slowly, slowly the knife was lowered—put aside.***

Figure 3: Text excerpt for Activity 13. May be photocopied for classroom use. © 2016 *Into the Story 2: More Stories! More Drama!* by Carole Miller and Juliana Saxton. Bristol, UK: Intellect.

Here is your task. In your groups, you are to cast the scene: characters you have to work with are the grandfather, the girl, the villager with the knife and others, as needed. We know the end of the story: ***And the three turned and walked towards the sea.*** Who those three are is up to you; what happens between the dropping of the knife and ***walking towards the sea*** is up to you. What you work out will be the way in which you want the story to end.

Figure 4: Instructions for Activity 14. May be photocopied for classroom use. © 2016 *Into the Story 2: More Stories! More Drama!* by Carole Miller and Juliana Saxton. Bristol, UK: Intellect.

Chapter Eight

Mary Ellery, Traveler in Space

From a text created by Norah Morgan, based on the Ann Graham lesson of Jonothan Neelands

Why Did We Choose This Story?

- This is a very, very short story. There are no illustrations. We chose this text because the activities are designed to enable the creating of a story that belongs to the whole class. They are truly the authors of the story's unfolding. In that unfolding, many strategies and techniques may be used to tap into the power of the collective imagination.
- The questions posed open up the possibilities of both the narrative and the subtext, moving beyond questions that simply ask for information (often based on a personal assumption of "what happened").
- As the class fills in between the lines of the plot, they address concerns of feelings and opinion that help us to understand what happened and why it might have happened in that way.
- The exploration of the text through thoughtful, creative and critical ways helps us to think about the implications of choices, decisions and actions and the ethical constructs that underlie them.

Key Understandings and Questions

- Whose contributions to history have disappeared or been erased?
- What reasons would cause someone to disappear from history?
- What might be the motivations for keeping a secret?
- There are many reasons for choosing not to remember something.

1. Commemoration: remembering visually — ***20 minutes***

Grouping:	**Groups of eight or nine**
Strategy:	**Tableau / transforming**
Administration:	**Text displayed on OHP or other media; sentence strips (two per group); felt pens**
Focus:	**To interpret the source after and before the voyage**

Teacher puts up/reveals the source.

Teacher: Just read this fragment quietly to yourselves. [They do]

In the year 2050, Mary Ellery, daughter of William and Elizabeth Ellery, left her home in Mountsville to travel to the planet Osiris. She was a member of the group Venture, led by Dr. James Harvey. Mary never returned. The team does not speak of her. There is no mention of her in the records and her name does not appear in the medal citation that honours the work of Dr. Harvey and his group.

Move into groups of eight or nine. Find a space in the room where you can work independently. [They do]

In your group and based on your reading of the story, create the photograph of the group Venture which was taken *on its return* and is the "Photo of Record" that appears in the historical records of space travel in the twenty-first century. In your picture we will, of course, see Dr. Harvey. I am not sure where you will place him but we will know who is Dr. Harvey by the ways in which the rest of the group relate to him. We are looking for subtlety here but you will have to work quickly. [They do]

As they are working, teacher gives a felt pen and two sentence strips to each group. After three to five minutes,

Teacher: Please stop now. What might be the words that appear under the photograph? Just take a minute to decide and then, using the sentence strip, record your decision. [They do]

Thank you. In your group and based on your re-reading of the source, now create the photograph that was taken of the group Venture *before* the team set out on its expedition to Osiris. Again, we will know how the group relates to Dr. Harvey.

After three to five minutes,

Teacher: What might be the text that appears under this photograph? [They write]

You now have two photographs or what we call in drama, tableaux. With tableaux, you can play with them in all sorts of ways. Here, we would like you to create a way in which the first tableau ("the return") moves into the picture of the group *before* it set out. We are moving slowly, dissolving/transforming from photo one back to photo two. Obviously, you will have to make some decisions. [They do]

Now that you have choreographed that movement, and have it in memory, do the "run" again so that it flows from photo one ("the return" to photo two "before departure") and back to photo one. You need to remember to incorporate your sentence strips, this time orally so that we can all hear as well as see. Decide how you will do this. [They do]

Note: Sometimes students will take photos on their digital media. It is always interesting to see if and how they may use those photos later. After enough time to practice,

Teacher: Let's share these photographs and captions now. Just make sure you can see from where you are.

Those who are observing, close your eyes. When the group is ready and still, I will say, "Open" and you will see and hear each as they transform from one to another and back again.

No talking; just look carefully.

Each group presents without discussion.

Teacher: Just sit down and talk together about what you have seen and heard. [They do]

After a minute or two,

Teacher: The work we are about to do is to investigate the events that occurred between the embarkation of Venture and its return and what led to the erasure of Mary Ellery from the records.

2. What can we learn from the text? ***15 minutes***

Grouping: **Whole class**
Strategy: **Deconstructing a text**
Administration: **Text written out on chart paper or projected**
Focus: **To discover what we know from the text**

Teacher: Today we are going to explore the ways in which people make stories together—to see what happens when we lay our stories alongside other people's. This means that we are all going to listen very carefully so that no one imposes his or her story on the story we are *all* making. Let me be very clear about one thing;

the story we make *is* the story. Don't come up to me at the end and say "Yes, but now tell us the *real* story" because the real story is the one we will make. The only thing we have to build our story from is this fragment.

Just read the text again quietly to yourselves. [They do]

What do we know from reading this? What are the facts?

An example of a conversation:

Student A: Mary Ellery died on this exploratory trip.
Student B: We don't know that she died or if she died, if it was on the trip.
Student A: You're right!
Student C: She lived in Mountsville.
Student D: She must have disappeared under strange circumstances because no one talks about her.
Student E: We don't know that; people may not have spoken about it because they were told not to.
Student F: I wonder how many people were members of that group? (And so on)

3. What questions do we have? 20 minutes

Grouping: **Groups of five**
Strategy: **Building questions and assumptions**
Administration: **Six sheets of chart paper; six felt pens**
Focus: **To sort out assumptions from facts; to work collectively; to consider the most effective means of phrasing questions**

Teacher: We really don't know very much, do we? What questions are beginning to form in your mind? What do we need to know?

OPTION

The following information may be useful if students have difficulty formatting open questions that lead to greater possibilities for the drama.

Teacher: There are really only three basic kinds of questions, although there are many ways of asking them.

The first kind, of course, is a question that *asks for information*. And often, that is very important. However, we need to discover how we can word our questions so that they open up the possibilities of both the narrative and the subtext—what lies under the story. For example: Who were Mary Ellery's parents? Who was the leader of the *Venture*?

The second kind of question is one that seeks to *fill in between the lines* of the plot, that taps into feelings and opinions and helps us to understand not only what happened but why it might have happened in that way? For example: What motivates someone to travel into space? How did Mary's parents respond to her ambitions?

Finally, we need to word our questions in thoughtful, creative and critical ways that help us to *think about the implications* of what has happened or what may happen. For example: What reasons might there be for eradicating the contributions of some to the stories of our history? We are thinking here of Tiananmen Square or other recent historical events where erasure or silence may have played a part.

Teacher may want to record these kinds of questions on the board or project them for reference.

If students are already aware of the different kinds of questions, pick up the work here.

Teacher: Groups of five, please. Take a sheet of chart paper and one felt pen per group. Appoint a secretary to record your questions. [They do]

You will need to listen carefully to each other and be aware of swamping other people's ideas with your own. We are working out of the facts we have and any logical assumptions that arise from those facts. You have about five minutes.

Students work by discussing, arguing about the relevance, the wording and the importance of the questions. The teacher stands aside and reminds them of time passing (which can be nearer ten minutes than five).

Teacher: Right everyone. Stop there. Order the questions so that you agree on those that are most important. [They do]

Let's hear what we've got from each group in turn. Who's ready to begin? [Group A so indicates]

Questions are shared. Teacher records those questions that the class agrees upon on the board, next to the source. An example of conversation:

Group A: What branch of the government was the team working for?

Teacher: Be careful! You are imposing your own story. We don't know enough yet to make an assumption like that. Can you word the question another way so that that information could be revealed?

Group A: To whom did Dr. Harvey report?

Group C: No, that's still not right. You're assuming that Dr. Harvey had a boss. We've got a better one! Who was funding the *Venture* group? (*information* question)

Teacher: Are we agreed that that will be a useful question? [They agree]

The sharing continues until there are between 10 and 15 questions that the whole class agrees are useful. Throughout, careful consideration is given to how the questions are phrased. Some examples of teacher prompts,

- How could we put it another way so that it will help us to open up the inquiry rather than close it down?
- Can we write that question another way so that it gets at what we want to know more directly? Remember we want to keep the story very open at this point.
- Try not to follow one plot line but rather make these questions so that they open up a lot of possibilities.

4. Who holds the answers to these questions? ***20 minutes***

Grouping: **Whole class**

Strategy: **Discussion**

Administration: **Groups' questions, felt pens**

Focus: **To build a collective list of questions that are useful, well-phrased to elicit information and congruent with the period of the source; finding roles**

Teacher: Read the questions we have listed. As you are reading, ask yourself the following: Who might be able to answer them? Who might help us to understand what really happened to Mary? We are looking for the roles that will help us to discover the missing plot information and a better understanding of those events.

The class offers suggestions: An example list:

- One or both of Mary's parents (*Parents know their children in different ways*)
- Dr. John Harvey
- A member of the Venture group

It may be necessary to remind students to seek more widely in order to explore all possibilities.

- The person who conferred the medal

If students object, it may be useful to rephrase, for example:

> "What I'm hearing is that you also want to speak to people not involved with the mission who might know something simply because of their positions."

Students add:

- The Venture's recorder or log keeper
- The team's physician
- Mary's boyfriend

This last suggestion is narrow; it may be helpful to suggest that this could be "I" writing rather than "we" writing, and to remind students to "Remember we are building our story collectively." In "I" writing, someone is trying to control the narrative, often in order to make a "juicy" story; in "we" writing, we build on what we have heard to create a collective story—which does not deny the juicy possibilities.

- Someone close to Mary
- Mary's teacher (*Teacher asks:* "A teacher from which part of Mary's life would hold the most important information for us?")

As the roles are approved they are listed on the board/chart paper beside the 10–15 questions.

<u>**Teacher:**</u> Now we have a number of people (eight to nine) who might be able to give us some answers that would help us to build our story. As you think about what has happened today, be careful not to build a story of your own. This does not mean that you cannot imagine, but we need to be able to believe in the logic of the story. For example, if as Mary's teacher, you state that she was a loner, we may hear later that she did, in fact, have a boyfriend but kept that relationship secret. Remember, the story we are building is one that must belong to all of us. Thank you for your hard work.

5. Reconnecting with the text — ***5 minutes***

Grouping: **Whole class**

Strategy: **Silent reading**

Administration: **Questions and roles transcribed onto chart paper and pinned up by text**

Focus: **To review information and set the tone for serious work (*this is important if the work is to happen on a later day*)**

<u>**Teacher:**</u> Everyone, please re-read the text that we have been investigating and examine the questions we developed and the people we decided might be able to provide answers. We need to have this information at our fingertips as this is going to be a very demanding part of our work. [They do]

There may be some quiet conversation while they are reading.

6. Who will we talk to and how are we going to do it? ***5 minutes***

Grouping:	**Whole class—divided (see below)**
Strategy:	**Organizing or "setting the stage"; enough chairs for each student**
Administration:	**Chairs set in a circle; five chairs to be placed randomly**
Focus:	**To be sure each student knows "what's up"**

Teacher: We need to deepen our understanding of the events surrounding the disappearance of Mary Ellery and for that I am going to invite five volunteers to help us. Each volunteer will take on the responsibility of representing one of the roles we have listed on the board. [Five students offer]

Someone may ask why fewer people than roles, to which the answer is that there needs to be choice for the participants taking on roles, as they see how the story unfolds.

Teacher: Thank you. I am going to ask you to stand apart from us. Please *do not talk* to each other. And, while I know that you are prepared to undertake one of the roles listed, please *do not make* that choice now. I will tell you the reason for that and what we are going to do in a moment.

Teacher turns to class,

Teacher: The rest of you, please arrange your chairs in a circle. [They do]

Teacher places five empty chairs randomly within the circle, facing in different directions.

Teacher to the role players:

You will come in when you are called, sit on any chair you choose. Once you sit, you are in role. Do not decide which role you will take now but make up your mind which role you think might be the most useful for us to hear from, *as you are coming in*. You will need to listen very carefully to each interview because we are building a story together. That does not mean that your role may not have a different point of view; for example, if Mary's father were to be interviewed and tells us that Mary's mother died shortly after Venture returned, that would be a fact that would become a part of the story and a role that is now not available to us. But if Dr. Harvey says that Mary's father did not want her to join Venture, that is something with which you, as Mary's father might want to disagree.

The reason why I ask you not to decide on your role beforehand is because as the interviews proceed, you may see that one role from our list of roles, rather than another, would be more helpful. Remember that in drama girls can play men and boys can play women. We are looking for believable attitudes and points of view that can help us build our story.

Teacher to everyone: We are ready now to question. The questions that we have created are important but a response may trigger a different question, so do not feel constrained by our list.

We will all have to listen carefully to the answers we are given because it is upon those answers that we will begin to understand what may have happened.

Remember two very important things: the people we are going to meet have *agreed* to speak to us. But we need to remember that *over 10 years have passed* since Mary's disappearance.

Here the teacher is beginning to indicate that those who are to question are in a fringe role of people who have the right to ask these questions.

Teacher: I know you will treat these people with respect and that you understand that memory is not always to be relied upon.

7. Who will we meet and what will they tell us? ***20 minutes***

Grouping: **Five class members to take on roles; class members in outer circle**

Strategy: **Hot seating**

Administration: **As set out above**

Focus: **To develop questioning skills; to fold new information into old; to encourage focused listening; to work in role**

Teacher to the students sitting in the circle:

Thank you for coming today to try and solve the mystery of Mary Ellery's disappearance. We are here to find the truth and I know I do not need to remind you that we have all signed the form agreeing that we will not publish our findings without permission.

Teacher is in a fringe role, the students in a general role that will give them a reason for asking the questions.

Teacher: It is important to remember that the event we are investigating happened *10 years ago*. There will, therefore, be things that our guests will not be able to remember, things that they simply do not wish to talk about and, perhaps, things that they cannot talk about.

Using a gesture only, the teacher invites someone in the "role group" to come forward into the circle and sit down in one of the chairs.

Teacher: Thank you for coming. May I ask your name and your relationship to or connection with Mary Ellery?

An example of the procedure:

Student (*in role*): My name is William Ellery. I am Mary's father.

Teacher: We know you might find some of our questions distressing and that you may have forgotten some of the details of that time ten years ago. We will understand if you do not wish to answer all the questions. This is not an inquisition.

Teacher turns to the wider circle and invites,

Teacher: Who has the first question for Mr. Ellery?

The teacher follows the same format with the other four students. Examples: the team's physician; a member of the Venture team; Dr. Harvey; the medal presenter. It is important to note that while students in role are being questioned, they are not to interact with one another. For example, should Dr. Harvey make a derogatory comment about the medal presenter and s/he turns to say something:

Teacher: We are speaking to Dr. Harvey.

There will be a chance later for more general conversation, but at this point, it is important to keep the focus on the student in role who is being questioned. Generally there are about ten questions per role, although someone may have fewer questions because s/he tends to "gossip" more, whereas someone else may have more questions because s/he only answers what is asked of her. Some reasons for teacher intervention: clarification, curiosity, to rephrase in order to open up, and/or to change the pattern of the asking. Some examples of students' questions:

To Mr. Ellery: How did Mary describe her relationship with Dr. Harvey?

A good open question provides a number of pieces of information upon which others build their questions.

To the member of the team: And what kind of work did Mary do?

This question invites the team member to support or oppose what a previous speaker has implied.

To the team's physician: What do you think of Dr. Harvey?

This question seeks information but the way the question is framed allows for opinion as an answer that may not be very useful.

After the first round of questions,

Teacher to the circle of questioners:

I expect that now there are other questions in your minds that you would like to ask. Take a moment to think about what we now know and what you still need to discover.

8. Checking out the story ***10 minutes***

Grouping:	**Five students remain in role and in place; class seated in a circle as before**
Strategy:	**Questioning**
Administration:	**As above**
Focus:	**To ask the questions not yet asked; to check out the facts that do not seem to be consistent; to weave the story more tightly**

Teacher: These people (*indicating the five students in role in the centre of the circle*) will remain in role. You (*to other* *students*) may go around and ask them any other questions that you may have. Some of you may wish simply to listen in and gather information that may prompt you to ask further questions of someone else.

The group breaks up, moving among the chairs in the centre of the circle, asking questions or just listening to others asking questions. After about ten minutes,

Teacher: Thank you. We have no wish to tire these people out. They have been so helpful and patient putting up with our questions. (*To those in role*) You have given us a lot to think about. (*To the others*) Please return to your chairs.

9. What did we hear? ***5 minutes***

Grouping: **Whole class**
Strategy: **Reflection**
Administration: **Large circle of chairs**
Focus: **To share what has been learned; to evaluate its importance; to try and fit it into the story that is developing**

Teacher to the role players:

Please, come out of role now and bring your chairs back into the large circle. [They do]

Teacher to the whole group:

Has anyone picked up any new information that you feel you should share with us?

Interesting things will be mentioned, phrased in such ways as:

- I learned that …
- I don't understand why her …

- Dr. Harvey seemed uncomfortable about …
- I think we should all know that …
- I don't remember what the question was that got that answer…does anyone know?

10. The unheard voice — ***10 minutes***

Grouping:	**Whole class**
Strategy:	**Narration**
Administration:	**Chairs as above**
Focus:	**To arrive at an open conclusion; to discover if there is further interest in exploring the story**

After discussion and sharing of ideas,

Teacher narrates: Thank you. It is clear from this discussion that many people had their own ideas about what had happened to Mary. And some eighteen months later, based in part on our research, a Commission of Inquiry was appointed to look into The Matter of Mary Ellery. After many witnesses and much deliberation, the final decision of the commission investigating Mary's disappearance was that no one would ever know the truth. It was, however, the unanimous decision of the Commission that an injustice had been done in erasing Mary's name from the record and there is now a movement afoot to remedy this omission.

Thank you.

The lesson ends here with the following reflective possibilities. If the class would like to pursue the story further, please see suggestions below.

Teacher: Just take a moment to think about the story and the process we have been exploring. And when you are ready, turn to the people around you and talk about the ideas that we discovered about Mary Ellery and the whole business of this space venture.

Some questions:

I wonder what might be your concerns about it and why you feel that Mary needed to be erased from what appears to have been a successful expedition?

I am wondering if you can think of anyone or any peoples we now know about whose contributions to history seem almost to have disappeared?

The whole idea of "disappearance" has contemporary relevance.

What reasons might lead to someone disappearing from history?

What might be the motivations for keeping such a secret?

There will be a fair bit of buzz as students talk together. Take some time for this debriefing before bringing the group together to share ideas and thoughts.

Note: Working in drama, it is important to talk about the drama world first before you move into a reflection on the power of questions to open up stories. Here we can explore why such questions are important for learners to know how to ask, and what new questions now arise.

Teacher: Thinking back to what we all now know, what, for example, were the critical questions that seemed to move us, and the drama, along?

Writing and design extensions

- In groups of five, using these pens and large sheets of paper, what suggestion or suggestions would you have for a fitting way to remember Mary?

- Write the missing entries in the log that would have recorded what happened when Mary disappeared.
- Choose an entry from Mary's diary that might have proven to have significance in solving the mystery of her disappearance.
- In either two or three dimensions, choose an appropriate medium and design the memorial to the Osiris expedition (see Resources below).

Further drama activities

Teacher: Of course, one of our difficulties in making this story is that we have never met Mary and only know of her through others. Because we are working in drama, we can move back and forward in time and so, if you would like, we could have an opportunity to hear from Mary.

Based on what we have been thinking and talking about, there seem to be a number of issues to which Mary might be able, or want to respond. Here are some suggestions and after you have read through them, you might want to suggest others.

The prompts below are guides only. Add any prompts that students offer and that the group recognizes to have potential. Use media to keep these prompts available. Ask students what strategies might be suitable for exploring Mary's answers.

- Had you, Mary, been able to speak to the results of the Commission's findings, what statement would you have wanted to place in the record?
- If you, Mary, could speak to any one of the people we met, to whom would you choose to speak and what would you say to him or her?
- How do you, Mary, want to be remembered?
- Mary, if you could write your own epitaph on the memorial, what would you want to see inscribed there?
- [Student suggestions ...]

OR

Students may wish to build a list of questions to put directly to Mary and to which they can refer during the following strategy:

Mary's voice	***10 minutes***
Grouping:	**Four student volunteers; remaining students**
Strategy:	**Group hot seating**
Administration:	**Four chairs at the front, enough chairs in a half circle for the rest of the class**
Focus:	**To hear how Mary's perspectives add to the story**

Teacher: Of course, one of our difficulties in making this story is that we have never met Mary and only know of her through others. Because we work in drama, we can move back and forward in time and so, if you would like, we have an opportunity to hear from Mary.

If the students agree to meet Mary,

Teacher: I am going to put out four chairs here, facing the chair circle. [*S/he does*]

Are there four people who would be prepared to take on the role of Mary? [They volunteer]

Thank you. Please sit here. [*Indicates chairs*]

Although there will be four people in role as Mary, only one person needs to respond to each question. All four of you will have to listen very carefully in order to build on each other's responses. In this way, we will be able to deepen and extend our understanding of Mary Ellery and, perhaps, we will gain some other ideas that may shed some further light on these events.

Generally, the hot seating need go no longer than three or four minutes and there is no expectation that the "Marys" will solve (or resolve) the issue of her disappearance.

Teacher: Thank you. You have given us a lot to think about but there are still many questions to be answered. Now it is time for you to write about the story as *you* see it. Hold to the facts that have been established but you are free to tell the story in your own way and from the point of view that best matches your "take" on the events. You may write it as a diary entry, a letter, a short story, a newspaper article, or as the summary of a trial—in any way that you feel is right for what you want to say and how you want to say it.

And now we have moved on to a writing activity. Enjoy!

Materials

Activity 1: Text written out on chart paper or other media; sentence strips (two per group); felt pens
Activity 2: Text as above
Activity 3: Six sheets of chart paper; six felt pens
Activity 4: Groups' questions; felt pens
Activity 5: Questions; list of roles on chart paper; text
Activity 6: Chairs set out in circle; five chairs to be placed
Activity 7: As above
Activity 8: As above
Activity 9: All chairs in circle
Activity 10: As above

Resources

There are a number of useful websites. We suggest:

- www.arlingtoncemetery.mill/visitor.../Space_Shuttle_Challenger.html; www.seasky.org/spacexp/sky5a.html
- Google pages on war memorials, their significance and symbolism.

Morgan, N., & Saxton, J. (2004). A classification of questions. In *Asking better questions* (pp. 45–62). Markham, ON: Pembroke.

Chapter Nine

A Piece of Bread

Based on *Rose Blanche,* written by Roberto Innocenti and Christophe Gallaz

Why Did We Choose This Story?

- The understanding of an historical event remains distant until students can find connections between the event and their own lives.
- *Rose Blanche* is a story that offers opportunities to see the events that took place from a different number of perspectives. These provide an introduction to the complexities that underlie all events of significance.
- Told simply, the text leaves many spaces to be explored; the illustrations, equally clear and detailed, are rich with feelings that are accessible to all children and young people.
- Holocaust education is a component of many social studies curricula, as is World War II.
- The historical frame opens up opportunities for research, particularly for personal stories from grandparents and great grandparents.

Key Understandings and Questions

- How are political ideologies generated and how may they develop?
- How do leadership and ideology cause people to behave in ways that betray their humanity?
- The actions of one apparently powerless person can make a significant difference to the lives of many.

Note: In terms of the first activity, students may be aware that the Holocaust will provide the context of the lesson. However, you may choose to begin without framing the work specifically.

1. Building context ***15 minutes***

Grouping:	**Four to five groups (depending upon class size) divided equally**
Strategy:	**Brainstorming**
Administration:	**Large chart paper, one sheet for each group with a single word/phrase written in large letters in the middle of the page; felt markers; masking tape**
Focus:	**To build collaborative meanings**

Divide class into four or five groups, each group is given a large sheet of paper and a number of felt pens. Each sheet has one of the following words or phrase written on it in large print.

Groups	**Words**
Group A:	COLLABORATION
Group B:	RESISTANCE
Group C:	TURN A BLIND EYE
Group D:	COURAGE

Depending upon the size of the class and their experience in group work, you may wish to have smaller groups. If you feel your class works best in smaller groups, more than one group may interpret the same word.

Teacher: Write down any thoughts and images that come to mind as you look at the keyword or phrase on your page. It doesn't matter if you have ideas that are different. Build on each other's ideas. You will need to work quickly. [They begin]

There may be some talking. The talking helps to generate ideas. Remind students that they do not have much time to complete the task. Stop after two minutes or when you see that there are five or more words/phrases on each of the sheets.

Teacher: In a moment, I am going to ask you to move on to where the group next to you has been working.

When you get there, look at what the previous group has written and then add your ideas to the keyword. For example, Group A will add their ideas on "Resistance" to Group B's initial thinking. Group B will move to Group C's "Turn a blind eye", and Group C will move to Group D's "Courage"; Group D will move to Group A's "Collaboration" and so on.

Ready? Off you go. [They do]

After each group has added their ideas to the original, the groups move on again. The rotation is completed when each group has added their "take" to the other sheets of paper and returned to their original word.

Teacher: Look at the new ideas that have been added by other people to your original comments. Talk about these and how your ideas have been expanded. [They do]

Students read the additions to their thinking and talk about what has been added. This conversation is critical for the next strategy.

2. Making abstract concepts concrete ***15–20 minutes***

Grouping: **As above**

Strategy: **Tableau**

Administration: **A working space for each group**

Focus: **Using their bodies to convey meanings that are basic to the story**

Teacher: Take the essence of what is on your page and what you have talked about and, using everyone in your group, create a tableau that best represents your thinking about your keyword or phrase.

This is going to be difficult because you have so many wonderful ideas. You are going to have to make some decisions about how you can represent those ideas in a still picture, a tableau.

We are going to be reading these tableaux just as we read the words on your pages. Therefore, you need to be sure that you can hold the picture still for us while we read it.

You will need to work quickly. You have about three minutes.

Students may need more time, but it is better to limit their time to begin with and give another minute when necessary.

When the students have their tableaux prepared, arrange groups in a circle so that all can move from picture to picture around the circle.

Teacher: Just before we begin to share, let's hang up the keyword collages. They will be a reference for our work now and later. [They do]

As the group is getting ready to present, I will tell everyone else to close their eyes while they prepare. When I say "Open", you may open your eyes and begin to read the picture. I will remind you of the word that is being interpreted.

As each tableau is presented (about one minute for each),

Teacher: What do we see?
Where do you see this?

Student observers offer their ideas. An example:

Student: I see tension.
Teacher: Where do you see that?

Student: In the position of his arm.

<u>Teacher:</u> Where else might we see tension?

We are asking the students to say what they see and where they see it (reading the picture); to identify for all of us the specific clues that read "tension"; then, and only then, to consider the possible interpretations.

<u>Teacher:</u> Thank you very much. Those were powerful tableaux and have helped us to understand what we all are thinking about when we hear the words that we have been working with.

How we understand those words is going to be very important to us as we enter our story.

Where do we see these ideas reflected in our own lives? [They share]

Depending on time, this might be the end of the first class. If not,

Now, I think we are all ready to enter the story. I'm going to read the first page and I'd like you to think about how the words we have been investigating may connect.

<u>3. Meeting Rose</u> ***<u>2 minutes</u>***

Grouping: **Whole group**

Strategy: **Reading aloud**

Administration: **Text of *Rose Blanche;* OHP or other media of the first picture**

Focus: **Introducing the context; gathering information**

<u>Teacher reads page one and shows picture:</u>

Look at this picture as carefully as you looked at the tableaux. What do you see?

As the students examine the picture, teacher side coaches:

What is the mood?
What might be the relationship of the soldiers on the truck to the civilians?
What do you think is going on?
Who are some of the people?

Teacher: Who in the picture do you think is Rose?

There may be some negotiation that can lead into a brief discussion about how artists focus the viewer's eye. When Rose is identified,

Teacher: If we agree that she is Rose, can we all agree that the woman who is just behind her is her mother?

This agreement is central to the next task.

Teacher: What might we want to know about Rose's mother? What sort of questions might we have for her?

It may be useful to write these questions on the board or chart paper as guides.

4. Meeting Mrs. Blanche ***8 minutes***

Grouping: **Three student volunteers**
Strategy: **Hot seating**
Administration: **Three chairs at the front; enough chairs in a half circle for the rest of the class**
Focus: **Entering the global event through the perspective of one woman's personal situation**

Teacher: I am going to put out three chairs facing the chair circle. [*S/he does*]

Are there three people who would be prepared to take on the role of Mrs. Blanche? We are looking for Mrs.

Blanche's attitudes and ideas so gender is not an issue. [They volunteer]

Thank you. Please sit here. [*Indicates chairs*]

Although there will be three people in role as Mrs. Blanche, only one person will respond to each question. All three of you will have to listen very carefully in order to build on each other's responses. In this way, we will be able to learn and extend our understanding of what is happening in the lives of these people.

What questions do we have for Mrs. Blanche?

Teacher as part of the group may become a questioner in order to model, to enlarge the range of possibilities or to embed tension.

Modeling: Mrs. Blanche, can you tell us what brings you and your daughter to the town square?
Enlarging: Mrs. Blanche, when did your husband decide to enlist or was his decision made for him?
Embedding tension: As a mother, how do you explain all of this to your daughter?

Generally, the hot seating need go no longer than three or four minutes. Having heard the responses of Mrs. Blanche, the reflection on the hot seating activity is embedded in the next strategy.

5. Describing Rose — ***5 minutes***

Grouping: **Whole group**
Strategy: **Role on the wall**
Administration: **A life-size cut-out of Rose laid out on the floor; felt pens (except for black)**
Focus: **Formulating opinions and making assumptions from very little information**

Teacher:	Having learned something about Mrs. Blanche and met Rose and her mother in the town square, what words would you use to describe Rose?

The life-size form of a child approximately four feet tall is placed on the floor.

Teacher:	If you think you have an idea or an adjective that will describe Rose, come and write it somewhere on the outline. Let's start by hearing some possible ideas.

As students offer, invite them to come and write.

Teacher:	There are lots of pens here, come up when you are ready.

When a number of words have been contributed,

Teacher:	Who is willing to read out some of these words? Listen for any contradictions and if you feel something might be missing, please just add it. [They hear] We'll just hang our descriptions of Rose on the wall as a reminder. While I'm doing this, each of you take piece of paper and pencil and find your own space in the room.

6. Another perspective ***7 minutes***

Grouping:	**Whole group**
Strategy:	**Guided imagery; writing in role**
Administration:	**Paper and pencils; OHP or other media of the first picture**
Focus:	**Seeing the story from the soldiers' perspective**

If possible, lights should be dimmed.

Teacher: Let's examine this picture again. Look at the soldiers in the truck. Keep this picture in mind and close your eyes.

Note the use of "you" to indicate a change in role.

Imagine that you are one of these soldiers. As you notice, some of you are very young. Some of you may be fathers, husbands or brothers. For some of you this will be your first time away from home and from your town. You've been riding in that truck for almost eight hours.

It is now late at night and you are lying in your bunk. You are the only one awake. You can't sleep. Your thoughts return to home, to those you've left behind. Who is that one person whose voice you hear within you, whose voice you can't get out of your mind?

To whom are you writing? When you have decided, begin to write your letter. [They do]

Note: You are looking for about half a page of writing. Don't worry if students stop to think; the fact that others are still writing will be a stimulus to return to the task. When most students seemed to have finished,

Teacher: Finish up the sentence you are writing.

If this is the end of the class,

Teacher: Fold your piece of paper in half. On the outside write the name of the person to whom you were writing and put your distinguishing mark somewhere. This may be your name, family crest, identification number or a private mark that would be recognized only by the recipient. [They do]

7. Reconnecting ***5 minutes***

Grouping:	**Individual**
Strategy:	**Reading**
Administration:	**Students' letters**
Focus:	**Rebuilding connections to the story; re-meeting themselves in role; synthesizing their feelings and ideas**

If this is the next class: As students enter the room, they see their letters and pencils placed around the floor.

Teacher: Go and sit by your letter. Open the letter. Read it and let the power of your words recall the feeling of that first night alone in an unfamiliar place.

Now, read it again and find the one sentence or phrase that best expresses the feelings and thoughts you were experiencing as that soldier. When you find it, underline it. Commit that phrase or sentence to memory. [They do]

Or if the work is continuing:

Teacher: Read what you have written and find the one sentence or phrase that best expresses the feelings and thoughts you were experiencing as that soldier. When you find it, underline it. Commit that phrase or sentence to memory. [They do]

8. The soldiers' voices ***5 minutes***

Grouping:	**Whole group**
Strategy:	**Voice collage**
Administration:	**Students' letters**
Focus:	**To listen to a wide range of thoughts, feelings and ideas**

Teacher: Close your eyes. I am going to move among you. When you feel my hand on your shoulder, speak the words you have underlined aloud. We are building collective understanding and so we need to hear everyone's voice clearly.

When you have finished, lower your head so that I know that you have spoken.

Teacher moves through the room randomly. Leave your hand on the student's shoulder until s/he has finished speaking. A firm but gentle touch encourages speech. After the students have contributed, leave some space for silent reflection (30–60 seconds).

Teacher: Talk quietly to the person next to you about what you heard. [They do]

The following is an optional question and depends on the buzz of talk.

Who has something they would like to share?

But fighting a war is not just about what happens at the front. Listen to how it affects some of the people left behind.

9. The heart of the story — ***5 minutes***

Grouping:	**Whole class**
Strategy:	**Story reading**
Administration:	**Text of *Rose Blanche*; the picture of the children behind the wire on OHP or other media**
Focus:	**To explore the content of the story**

Teacher reads from page one (repeat) … to … ***Suddenly electric barbed wire stopped me.***

Teacher shows the accompanying picture. It is important to be sure that all students are able to see it and to have time to take it in.

10. At the fence ***5–7 minutes***

Grouping: **Students (as many as volunteer) at the fence**

Strategy: **Tableau; improvisation**

Administration: **None**

Focus: **To discover how something as simple as a fence can change your place in the world**

Teacher: Would some of you be willing to become the children behind the barbed wire fence? Would you be willing to become that picture? Who will volunteer to be some of those children? [They volunteer]

Position yourselves as the children in the picture. [They do]

The rest of you, look at what has been created and make any adjustments that you feel are needed. [They do]

Teacher is using tableau as a technique to provide a starting frame for the meeting about to take place.

Teacher to students not in the tableau:

Who of you are willing to become Rose Blanche? As in meeting Mrs. Blanche, we will have three of you play Rose. Remember, in drama gender is not an issue. [Three volunteer]

Rose, how close will you be to the fence? Each of you will need to find your own place in relation to the fence. [They do]

The rest of you will become the observers of what is about to happen. Watch and listen carefully. You, too, have a place in this scene.

Now, we are going to explore the conversation that may have taken place between Rose and the children at that very first meeting. Each Rose will contribute to the improvisation individually but as you are all representing Rose, you will need to listen to each other.

Observers, look at the tableau that has been created. We are writing this scene. From what you see, who do you imagine would speak first, Rose or one of the children? [They suggest]

What would that line be? [They suggest]

Examples: What are you all doing here?
Where did you come from?

Teacher: Who will say that line?
or
Which Rose will speak first? [The improvisation begins]

This should not be a long scene; a minute or two is enough. The improvisation is not designed to provide answers; its purpose is to raise the questions.

Teacher: Thank you. Just relax where you are.

Rose has just been witness to something that raises all sorts of thoughts and questions in her mind, some of which may make no rational sense. Nevertheless, they are her thoughts and feelings.

11. Trying to make sense of it all ***3–4 minutes***

Grouping: **Whole group divided into two lines**
Strategy: **Conscience alley**
Administration: **None**
Focus: **To reflect inside the drama**

Teacher: Will someone else now take on the role of Rose? You won't have to speak but you must listen very hard to what is being said. [Student volunteers] Thank you.

Will the rest of you make two lines, each facing the other and leaving enough room for Rose to walk between you.

We are going to hear Rose's thoughts and feelings as she walks away from that fence. Think of all of those thoughts and questions that she might have. What is in her mind as she walks away?

Teacher places Rose at one end of the line, reminding Rose that she will need to walk slowly so that everyone will have a chance to speak.

Teacher: As Rose walks down this road, away from the camp and the children, we hear what is going on in her mind. Make sure that Rose and all of us can hear what you have to offer.

Teacher may join a line to model.

Teacher: When you are ready, Rose, you may begin.

The student volunteer slowly walks from one end of the alley to the other. As s/he does, students on either side give voice to what they believe would be in Rose's mind. Some examples:

How did they get there?
Where are their parents?
Is this going to happen to me?
What did they do wrong?
I wonder if my mother knows?

Teacher: Thank you for your contributions and thank you, Rose. Is there anything anyone would like to say about that experience? [They share]

If "Rose" does not contribute, you may wish to ask if she heard anything that resonated with her.

Teacher: Think about what you've just heard as you join me for the rest of the story.

12. Sometime sense cannot be easily made ***3 minutes***

Grouping: **Whole class**

Strategy: **Story reading**

Administration: **Text of *Rose Blanche***

Focus: **To discover what happens**

Teacher reads from: … ***Suddenly electric barbed wire stopped me*** … to the end of the story.

Give students a few moments of silence to consider the impact of their work in relation to the story.

13. Reconsidering Rose ***2–3 minutes***

Grouping: **Whole class**

Strategy: **Revisiting role on the wall**

Administration: **Role on the wall; black felt pens**

Focus: **To compare what we thought and what has changed**

Teacher takes down the role on the wall and lays it on the floor along with black felt pens,

Teacher: What new information do we have that we can add to this child that would give us a better understanding of who she was?

Please add any words or phrases that will expand our new understanding of Rose.

Teacher may ask them to do this without talking, if it seems more appropriate.

14. Seventy years later **2 minutes**

Grouping:	**Whole class**
Strategy:	**Narration**
Administration:	**None**
Focus:	**To bridge time**

Teacher narrates:

It is now over 70 years since the time of the imprisonment of the children. You were those children. You are now adults. Some of you are husbands, wives, parents and grandparents and you have never forgotten Rose.

In commemoration of the 70th anniversary of your liberation, you make a pilgrimage to visit her grave. But it is not enough for you just to visit.

You need to speak to her again. What message will you leave for her?

15. "Hope lives when people remember"* (Simon Wiesenthal Center) *15 minutes

Grouping:	**Whole class working as individuals**
Strategy:	**Reflection in role; ritual**
Administration:	**Note cards, pencils/pens**
Focus:	**To find the words**

Teacher:

Take one of the note cards and a pen or pencil and find yourself a private place to gather your thoughts. Please leave a space in the centre of the room. [They do]

When you are ready, write what it is that you would like to say to Rose after all these years. [They do]

Give students enough time to synthesize and write their thoughts (about five minutes). While they are writing, the teacher takes the cut-out figure representing Rose and places it on the floor, plain side up. Perhaps, a box in the centre of the room, or some other suitable symbol to mark the grave may be used instead of the paper shape.

Teacher: Just take a moment to finish up and read over what you have written. [They do]

When you are ready, come up one by one, to Rose's marker, read your message aloud to her, leave it on her grave and return to your place.

When all have contributed, allow for further silence.

Teacher: Turn to the person next to you and talk together.

This conversation should not be guided in any way. Simply allow it to take place before inviting students to share their thoughts about the experience.

16. Making connections between past, present and future As long as needed

Grouping: **Whole class**
Strategy: **Reflection**
Administration: **None**
Focus: **To consider the implications of this event for themselves and for the world**

Teacher: This event happened a long time ago and thousands of miles away. I wonder what connections we might make between our work and our own world today? When in your own life might you have felt compelled to take a stand?

Working in drama, it is important to talk about the drama world first. In this way, the feelings generated by the work will inform the discussion as the key understandings and questions begin to unfold. Only then can everyone move into a reflection on the power of drama itself to open up stories, and talk about which strategies were of particular value to the process. The following quotations may be useful input for the reflective conversation.

Reflection prompts

> The world is a dangerous place to live … not because of those who do evil, but because of the good people who allow evil to happen.
>
> The Simon Wiesenthal Center

> … each and everyone of us can make a difference by not being indifferent.
>
> Henry Friedman,
> Holocaust Education Center, Seattle, WA

Materials

Activity 1: Large chart paper, one sheet for each group; felt markers; masking tape
Activity 3: Text of *Rose Blanche*; OHP or other media of the first picture
Activity 4: Three chairs at the front; enough chairs in a half circle for the rest of the class
Activity 5: Paper cut in the outline of a life-size child; felt pens (no black)
Activity 6: Paper and pencils; OHP or other media of the first picture
Activity 7: Students' letters
Activity 8: Students' letters
Activity 9: Text of *Rose Blanche*; the picture of the children behind the wire fence; OHP or other media
Activity 12: Text of *Rose Blanche*
Activity 13: Role on the wall; black felt pens
Activity 15: Note cards, pencils/pens

Resources

Innocenti, R. & Gallaz, C. (1985). *Rose Blanche*. Mankato, MN: The Creative Company.

Wall, V. (1993). A resource pull-out. *Drama: One forum, many voices*, 1(2) Spring, no pp.

Additional resources

Ackerman, K. (1995). *The night crossing*. New York, NY: Yearling.

Johnson, T. (2008). *The harmonica*. Watertown, MA: Charlesbridge.

Levine, K. (2003). *Hana's suitcase: A true story* (Reprint edition). Park Ridge, IL: Albert Whitman & Company.
Lowry, L. (1990). *Number the stars*. New York, NY: Yearling.
Pollacco, P. (2009). *The butterfly*. New York, NY: Puffin Books.
Zullo, A. (2005). *Survivors: True stories of children in the Holocaust*. New York, NY: Scholastic Paperbacks.

Chapter Ten

Aqua Pura

Based on *Beneath the Surface* written by Gary Crew and illustrated by Steven Woolman

Why Did We Choose This Story?

- *Beneath the Surface* is a book that raises all sorts of questions and provides very few answers.
- The illustrations are complex and evocative and often act as parallel stories that may or may not have something to do with the main text.
- Both text and illustrations make tremendous demands on the reader.
- There are many possibilities for integrating curriculum: environmental education, visual arts, social studies, composition, an examination of alien theories (Mars exploration and UFO theories) and in governance, issues of power and control.
- While the language is simple, the subtext encourages students to develop sophisticated literacy skills and critical analysis; the illustrations individually become sites for imaginative writing.

Key Understandings and Questions

- How does our community shape what we accept as "normal"?
- How do suspicions grow that all is not as it seems?
- What is the role of government in a time of environmental crisis?
- In a world where surveillance is becoming an accepted way to keep communities safe, what does the individual lose and what does s/he gain?
- In a world that is ecologically fragile, how do we balance the needs of the individual with the greater good of the collective society?

1. Preparing to enter the story ***7 minutes***

Grouping:	**Whole class**
Strategy:	**Drama exercise "Columbian Hypnosis" (Boal, 2002, p. 63)**
Administration:	**None (perhaps a tambourine as a signal)**
Focus:	**To build concentration and to respond exactly to a stimulus**

Teacher:

To get ready for our drama, we are going to do an exercise that will prepare us for the work that we are about to begin.

Find a partner and space where you can work together. [They do]

Decide who is A and who will be B. [They do]

The exercise we are about to do is called "hypnosis". What do you know about hypnotism? [They share]

As you will be the hypnotist. Bs you will be the hypnotized.

As your task is to hypnotize your partner by using only the palm of your hand. Hold your hand out a few centimetres away from the face of your partner. The tips of your fingers should be approximately at the hairline of your partner. Using only your hand, very slowly begin to move it either up or down, side to side, backwards and forwards.

Bs your task is to keep the palm of your partner's hand always the same distance away from your face and at the same level. As your partner moves his/her hand, you must follow using your whole body.

Let's just try this out for a moment. Hypnotists, don't move from your place, just see what happens. [They do]

Remember to use control so that your partner can follow closely. This exercise is not about trying to trick someone but rather, about having them follow your lead.

The challenge for both partners is to do this without any talking at all.

Let's start again. Partners, take your positions. [They do]

And begin.

This exercise should last about 30 seconds to a minute, depending upon focus.

Talk to your partner about that. [They do]

What advice would you give to improve your hypnotic skills? [They share]

Right. Change roles. Taking into account your experience in the other role, let's try this again. This time, work for the flow of the movement, keeping the idea of hypnosis in mind. You may move out of your space but be sure not to lose the connection with your partner and to keep your partner safe.

You may want to use some gentle music as a way of helping students to slow down and control their actions.

Stop now. Just talk your partner about that. What differences did you notice? What made it easy for you to follow? For you to lead? [They chat]

Why would someone choose to hypnotize another?

This exercise was developed by a famous theatre practitioner, named Augusto Boal. He used it as part of his program called Theatre of the Oppressed. I wonder why he would choose an exercise like this for his work with people who are oppressed?

This discussion should be brief but open to the whole group.

2. Building a background for understanding ***10 minutes***

Grouping:	**Whole class**
Strategy:	**Brainstorming**
Administration:	**A large roll of paper (suggest 3" x 10") on which is written two or three times along the expanse of the paper the phrase "The mind has a thousand eyes"; felt pens**
Focus:	**To generate ideas and build collaborative meanings**

Teacher: Those ideas that we just discussed may influence your ideas for the next part of our work.

Come and sit around this large piece of paper. [They do]

It is important for students to work with many different people. The ideas generated in the earlier exercise will have wider dissemination.

Teacher: On the paper in front of you is a line of poetry: "The mind has a thousand eyes". Close your eyes and listen to that phrase again. [*Teacher repeats the phrase twice*] What images or words come into your mind as you reflect on that saying?

Give students thinking time to consider what for them may be a sophisticated phrase.

Teacher: When you are ready, pick a felt pen and begin to write or draw your ideas. [They do]

Judge the time by the response. You may wish to encourage students to read what is being written around them in order to generate new ideas.

Teacher: In a moment, I'm going to ask you to put down your pen. So finish up what you are writing or drawing and pass the pens down to me. Thank you.

3. Sharing our collective ideas *2 minutes*

Grouping: **Whole class**
Strategy: **Voice collage**
Administration: **As above**
Focus: **To generate ideas and build on collaborative meanings**

Teacher: Now we are ready to hear our collective interpretations of the phrase, "The mind has a thousand eyes".

Just stand and turn to your right. Make sure that everyone has room to see the paper. You are going to move around that paper and you will need to remember what your learned in the previous exercise about keeping space between you.

As we circle around the paper, speak aloud the words and phrases that resonate for you. Don't worry about multiple voices speaking at one time, as we are layering our ideas as we do in a collage.

If you see a drawing, how will you interpret that visual representation in words?

When you have returned to your original spot, just sit down.

Are we ready to begin? Good. [They circle and voice what they see]

Once everyone is sitting down,

Teacher: Just talk to your partner about what you have discovered about this phrase. [They do]

Who has something they would like to share with the whole group?

Students may want to talk about the how of what they were doing, as well as about what they discovered.

Teacher: Thank you, you will find all these ideas and thoughts you have shared have much to do with our story.

In this story, eyes are an important symbol. We look out of them and others look into them.

4. Reflecting on what we have done ***10 minutes***

Grouping: **Whole group/pairs**

Strategy: **Reading aloud**

Administration: **The text *Beneath the Surface***

Focus: **Creating a context for listening**

Teacher: For the last little while, we have been preparing to enter the story. Each of the activities has built on the other, just as a playwright builds a play. Every play has an emotional context. Looking back at everything we have done to this point, what feelings seem to be present? What mood has been established?

There are no right or wrong answers but your comments will help to establish how we, as a group, move into the story. [They share]

As you listen to the first few lines of the story, keep those ideas in mind.

Note: In this story drama structure, only the text is shared, not the illustrations. The illustrations will be addressed in the extensions.

Teacher reads from the beginning of the story to ... ***he headed for the hotel.***

Now, find a partner and a place in the room to work.

<u>5. Spike's return</u> ***<u>10 minutes</u>***

Grouping:	**Pairs**
Strategy:	**Translating narration into dialogue**
Administration:	**The text of *Beneath the Surface* (pp. 4 and 5, see Figure 5); pencils for each student**
Focus:	**To move narration into dialogue**

<u>**Teacher:**</u> Find a partner and a place in the room to work.

As teacher is handing out text and pencils,

<u>**Teacher:**</u> Here is the next part of the story, the conversation between Spiro and the reception clerk. Read it silently to yourself and if you finish early, just think about what you have read. Don't talk about it yet. [They read silently]

Choose A and B.

A will be Spiro and B is the reception clerk. You will be reading this excerpt as dialogue from a scene in a play. That means we will hear only the conversation, not the narration. The narration serves as your scene direction. Is everybody clear about that?

Let's try reading the first two paragraphs as dialogue and see how we get on. [They do]

Any problems? [Students offer]

At this point, some students may be more successful at extracting the dialogue than others. Depending upon your objectives, you may want to address it. If not, don't make it an issue as it is all about engaging with the text.

<u>**Teacher:**</u> Start again and read through until the conclusion of the scene. But just before you do that, make a decision. Look at the last short paragraph. Will that paragraph be part of your dialogue? Or will you just think it? If so,

what words might you say to conclude the scene? You may add them. Ready? Begin.

It doesn't matter if they decide it is (or is not) part of the conversation, it is the decision-making that is important.

Teacher: When you have finished, talk together quietly about what you think might have happened to generate this conversation. [They do]

Change roles. [They do]

Read again. When you have finished, talk about other ideas that might have occurred to you during this second reading. [They do]

Now, let's take a moment to share some of your ideas. What sorts of things have your inferred from this conversation? What kind of story do you think this might be? [They share]

There is a key piece of information that students must be clear about and may not have raised in this sharing. If not, be sure to ask,

Teacher: Spiro says he is not a doctor of medicine but a scientist with a degree in hydrology. What might he be researching? [They respond]

6. The nightmare — *10–15 minutes*

Group: **Individuals**

Strategy: **Movement**

Administration: **Music (suggest: 30 Minutes of Horror Music: Atmospheric Soundtracks, Vol. 2, starting at 13:41, found on Youtube)**

Focus: **To explore Spike's inner world**

<u>Teacher:</u> I'm going to read you the last sentence from that section that you have been working on.

<u>Teacher reads:</u> ***He slept badly that night, his nightmares vivid and dreadful.***

I wonder what might be causing those nightmares and what might they be foreshadowing? I think it might help to hear the story again from the beginning.

<u>Teacher reads from the beginning</u> to … ***his nightmares vivid and dreadful.***

Talk to the person next to you about your ideas as to what might be disturbing Spike's sleep so badly.
[They do]

After a minute or two,

<u>Teacher:</u> Now, find your own space in the room. [They do]

Close your eyes and listen to this piece of music. As you listen, visualize in your mind's eye the kinds of feelings being generated by Spike's nightmare.

When you are ready, let the music and those feelings bring you to your feet and guide your movement. Express those vivid feeling and the dread he is experiencing through your movement. [They do]

If possible, lower the lights to create an ominous environment. Even without lighting, the music should take them into that other world.

<u>Teacher:</u> Thank you. Rest for a moment and then talk to the person next to you about what you imagined that nightmare to be. Is it possible to find the words?

Let them share for a few moments and then,

Teacher: Is there anyone who would like to speak about that experience? [They share]

Thank you. That experience will feed the rest of our drama.

7. Building the back story ***10 minutes***

Grouping: **Whole class**
Strategy: **Writing in role**
Administration: **Note cards; pencils**
Focus: **To concretize ideas about Spike**

Note: This next activity is a shift in tone and mood.

Teacher narrates: It doesn't take long for news to travel in a small town. By early the next morning, pretty well everyone knew that Spike Trotter was back. Those who didn't have email had telephones, maybe cell phones, and there was always the old-fashioned back fence.

Handing out note cards and pencils,

Teacher: On this note card, write to someone *who needs to know* about what you think might have brought Spike back? How might his return affect us all? Remember the day he and his mother left? What was that about? Have you heard about his degree in hydrology? What do you think he might be up to? [They write]

8. What are they saying? ***3 minutes***

Grouping: **Whole class**
Strategy: **Gossip mill**
Administration: **Note cards; pencils; tambourine**
Focus: **To work as an actor making choices for interpretation**

Teacher: Pick up your card and read those words over to yourself. Note which words you would be prepared to say aloud; underline and mark with an "A". Mark with a "W" anything that you would be prepared only to whisper. [They do]

Take a moment to commit those words to memory. [They do]

Let's try speaking or whispering those words out loud all together *and* all at once. [They do]

Sometimes it is a good idea to rattle the tambourine; this covering sound allows students to experiment with more confidence.

Teacher: Good. Put your card away.

Gather in the centre of the room. [They do]

When you hear the word, "begin", move around amongst each other speaking your sentence, phrase or words, using your own stage directions either to whisper or to speak aloud. You may want to use only one phrase but you may hear something where another of your choices would be more appropriate. In this gossip mill, we are creating a scene with our bodies and our words that is a concretization of the rumours that are enveloping our town.

Are there any questions?

Good. In a moment we will begin and when you hear the tambourine, freeze. Begin.

Give about 30 seconds for the students to "get the hang of it". After the tambourine,

Teacher: What were some things you heard that for you really caught the mood of the townspeople? [They share]

Let's try the gossip mill again, and now that we know the potential for this scene, see if we can find a way to build it. When it feels right, see if we can find a way to finish it that is both true to the mood we are creating and theatrically satisfying. [They repeat]

They may want to try this more than once. In which case, ask them what new things might be brought to it this time without dissipating the dramatic energy that will take them as listeners into the next strategy.

Teacher: Thank you. We now have a good idea of the atmosphere that Spiro's return has created in the townspeople. Let's read on.

9. The story ***5 minutes***

Grouping: **Whole class**

Strategy: **Reading aloud**

Administration: **Text of *Beneath the Surface***

Focus: **To listen for the plot**

Teacher reads from: ***He slept badly that night*** … to … ***and raising the vial to his lips, he drank.***

10. The beginning of the end (or vice versa?) ***10 minutes***

Grouping: **Groups of five or six**

Strategy: **Sculpting; tableaux with text; re-enactment**

Administration: **Clear space; caption strips; pens as needed**

Focus: **To interpret words into image**

Teacher: Now for something a little easier. Please get into groups of five or six. [They do]

Will someone in your group volunteer to be Spiro? [S/he does]

The rest of the group are to mould an image of Spiro as he "raises the vial to his lips" and drinks. As you do this, consider what sort of feelings Spiro might be experiencing? Try and put those feelings into your image. This shouldn't take you more than a minute or two but it is an important step as we find our ending.

Students work swiftly and when all groups appear to be ready,

Teacher: Sculptors, move away to the edges so that we can all see these Spiros.

After enough time for observation,

Teacher; Well done. Spiros, relax for a moment. Is there anything that anyone would like to share? [They share]

Thank you. Now, on the count of three, Spiros, freeze again in the position your group has set you in. Try to recapture those feelings as he drinks.

Teacher counts down slowly as Spiros freeze,

Teacher: As you are frozen, everyone listen to the next few lines. You will only hear them once, so close your eyes and listen hard.

Teacher reads: ***"Aqua pura," he breathed, reassured. "The very basis of life ..." And, raising the vial to his lips, he drank.***

Students will be familiar with what has just been read. Leave a moment of silence to focus their listening, before continuing,

Teacher reads: ***One sip, they allowed him. One sip only. Which was both his end and his beginning ...***

Keeping your eyes closed, what images were in your mind as you heard those final words?

After a few moments,

Teacher: Spiros, join your groups and share your images and ideas together. [They do]

Give them a minute or two, not too long,

Teacher: Now, the challenge. Your task, working as illustrators, is to create your final tableau. In order to do that, use the image of Spiro that you have just created as the beginning of your work. How will that image transform into your final illustration? Your tableau will include everyone in your group.

Some things you need to think about: Who are the "they"? Who could those people be who allowed him only one sip? You may need only one final illustration or you may need two. [They decide and create the group tableau/x]

After they have worked this out, add the final instruction,

Teacher: How will the concluding words of the text, "***Which was both his end and his beginning***" be used in your presentation to complement your image of Spiro in this moment? You may choose to write the words as a caption, speak them singly or in unison, as a collage, song or chant, or you may choose to write your own text or add it to the author's text in some way.

Work quickly and cleanly; we are almost at the end of the story. Use your intuitions; you will know what to do.

You may want to add after they have been working for a few minutes,

Teacher: This is a very open-ended activity and offers a multitude of interpretations. Don't worry about the final "product". What we are interested in seeing are the ideas you can offer as possibilities. This is a work in progress. How much more time do you think you will need? [They decide]

The teacher needs to consider the time available and the quality of the work being accomplished. Too much time does not generally result in better work.

11. Sharing the work ***15 minutes***

Grouping: **As above**
Strategy: **Presenting**
Administration: **Clear space**
Focus: **To discover possibilities of interpretation**

Teacher: In a moment, we will share your work in progress. It may be best if we can see your presentations one right after the other to get a sense of our collective interpretation. Then we can reflect together at the end of the sharing.

At the conclusion of the presentation/s,

Teacher: Talk to each other about what you have seen. [They do]

Some suggested questions for whole group reflection:

- What ideas did the presentations hold in common?
- What did you see that surprised or concerned you?
- What do we now know about that phrase, "which was both his end and his beginning"?
- Of course, all these ideas that we have shared act as metaphors for the ways in which we see the world and its future. How do you see your ideas shaping our worldview and its future?

This may be where you wish to end. If so, we suggest that before doing so, you might like to return to the key questions and use them to contextualize the work the studen ts have done into the wider context of today's world.

On the other hand, you may wish to have the students extend the work with a focused viewing of the illustrations.

Extension

What do the illustrations tell us? ***As long as needed***

Grouping:	**Whole class**
Strategy:	**Sharing the illustrations**
Administration:	**Text of *Beneath the Surface* (perhaps on a document camera)**
Focus:	**To weave the implications of the illustrations into the story**

Teacher: This is not the end of the story. Let's look at the pictures that the illustrator, Steven Woolman, uses to accompany the text.

Teacher may want to re-read the story as the illustrations are shown. In sharing the illustrations, note the insert drawings embedded in the illustrations as they tell the plot of the story.

Teacher: Talk together about what you think the story is really about? What is happening in the big pictures and what do you think the author and illustrator are telling you? Or warning you about?

In groups of between four and six, show us one scene of not more than two minutes in length that will give us some idea of what you think is at the heart of the story.

OR

> Individually (or in pairs) write a scene that shows us something that you feel is a part of this story. May I remind you of the last words, you might find them helpful?

These scenes can be documented and shared in multiple ways.

Materials

Activity 1:	Tambourine
Activity 2:	Large roll of paper (3" x 10") with "The mind has a thousand eyes" written in the middle of the page two or three times; felt pens
Activity 3:	As above
Activity 4:	Text of *Beneath the Surface*
Activity 5:	The text from pages four and five (see Figure 5); pencils for each student
Activity 6:	Music as suggested
Activity 7:	Note cards; pencils
Activity 8:	As above; tambourine
Activity 9:	Text of *Beneath the Surface*
Activity 10:	Caption strips available; pens as needed

Resources

Crew, G. (2004). *Beneath the surface.* Sydney, AU: Hodder Children's Books.

The following text is the precursor of *Beneath the Surface* and provides some of the back story to our drama:

Crew, G. (1997). *The watertower.* Flinders Park, AU: Era Publications.

Additional resources

Boal, A. (2002). *Games for actors and non-actors* (A. Jackson, Trans.). New York, NY: Routledge.

Bourdillon, F. W. (1895). The night has a thousand eyes. In E. C. Stedman (Ed.), *A Victorian anthology 1837–1895.* May be accessed from http://www.bartleby.com/246/979.html

Ewing, R., Miller, C., & Saxton, J. (2008). Drama and contemporary picture books in the middle years. In M. Anderson, J. Hughes, & J. Manuel (Eds.), *Drama and English teaching: Imagination, action and engagement* (pp. 117–134). Melbourne, AU: Oxford.

"Trotter?" the reception clerk said when he saw the name. "There was a kid name of Spike Trotter lived 'ere once. No relation?"

Spike looked up from the register. "Actually the name's Spiro Trotter," he said, avoiding the question. "Doctor Spiro Trotter".

"Ya haven't come to set up no clinic, 'ave ya?" the clerk said. "'Cause I'm tellin' ya now, there's no one sick around here. No, sir."

"I'm not a medical doctor," Spike assured him. "I'm a scientist. My degree is in Hydrology."

"Ah, that's different then … 'Cause like I said, there's no diseases in this town. No, sir. No doctors neither. Not since …"

"I'm very tired," Spike interrupted, "can I have the key to my room?"

"Anyway, that Trotter kid shot through years ago," the clerk muttered, handing him the key. "Him and his mother likewise. Just up and left. Lost contact with 'em we did."

Good, Spike thought, but said, pleasantly enough, "That's life. People move on. They change."

"They do. They certainly do," the clerk answered. "Bit like towns, 'eh?"

And worlds, Spike thought as he climbed the narrow stairs. *Even galaxies …*

Figure 5: Text for Activity 5 (from pp. 4 and 5 of *Beneath the Surface*, unpaginated). May be photocopied for classroom use.

Chapter Eleven

I Longs for Bloo Skys

Based on *Woolvs in the Sitee,* written by Margaret Wild and illustrated by Anne Spudvilas

Why Did We Choose This Story?

- The story deals with contemporary issues appropriate for investigation with older students. Although it is a picture book, it invites students into a disturbed and disturbing world.
- The illustrations highlight the perspective of a child and his view of the world through the use of shadow, tone and colour.
- Most students will have a means of finding a personal connection with the protagonist. Many of us have experienced those shadows in our own lives and long for the comfort of blue skies.
- There are many opportunities for decoding text, for interpreting meaning, for translating text into other artistic forms. The story taps into the multiple literacies available to students for finding meaning.
- The work of this story drama structure highlights these multiple aspects of literacy through experiential engagement with the text; the strategies that are introduced may be used as a means of integrating curriculum.

Key Understandings and Questions

- How do our environments create our world view?
- What motivates people to take a stand?
- Democracy requires resilience.
- The pleasure/burden of democracy is that it allows citizens to make changes.

1. Introducing the story ***5 minutes***

Grouping:	**Whole group**
Strategy:	**Prediction**
Administration:	**A bag; some tins of food; matches; torch; warm clothing; a note that says, "*I've gon looking for yoo. Yor frend Ben*"**
Focus:	**To create interest**

Teacher: Just come round this table and have a look at these artefacts. As you look, feel free to talk to the person next to you.

What do we see?

To whom could they belong?

What might these things tell us?

Thinking as authors, what kind of story can you imagine as you think about those artefacts? Does anyone have an idea they would like to share? [They do]

This strategy is intended to capture their interest and to get them thinking.

2. Who is Ben? ***7 minutes***

Grouping:	**Pairs**
Strategy:	**Decoding and reading text; Mantle of the Expert**
Administration:	**The text of *Woolvs in the Sitee* (pages one and two, see Figure 6)**
Focus:	**To discover what we know about Ben**

Teacher: Find a partner and sit down together. [They do]

I am going to give you a piece of writing. Your first task is to read it. Having seen the note, you will, of course, recognize the writer as Ben. [They do]

Everyone finished?

Note: If the first activity has been omitted,

Teacher: Perhaps it would help you to know that this was written by a boy named Ben.

Are there any words that you haven't been able to de-code? [They share]

Now, I am going to ask you to read it again but this time to read it again in role as if you were a professional who has been called upon to provide expertise in order for us to understand a little about the person who wrote it. What professionals might be called upon in this way? [They respond]

The helping professions, such as psychologists, social workers, teachers, therapists, medical personnel, school counsellors and so on, would all be appropriate.

Teacher: Choose one of those professions that you are prepared to work with. When you have decided, just write down the profession you have chosen at the top of the page. This time, as you read through the eyes of the profession you have chosen, you are reading in order to gain information about the writer. [They read]

Talk to the person next to you about the assumptions you are making about the boy, Ben, based on what you have read and what your professional expertise suggests. Here, of course, I am talking about such things that you may have noticed, such as cognitive development, emotional health, physical sense of security, self-esteem, family background and so on.

You may wish, as you talk together, to make some notes based on your professional reading of the material that could be useful to us in a minute. Just use the other side of the page of text. [They talk and make notes]

3. Concretizing our views of Ben ***10 minutes***

Grouping:	**Whole class**
Strategy:	**Role on the wall**
Administration:	**A life-size cut-out of young boy; felt pens**
Focus:	**To make evident our assumptions**

Teacher: I am now going to put down an outline that represents this young boy, Ben.

Having discussed your assessment, please come and write on this outline, the words or phrases that, as professionals, you would use to describe him. Many of your contributions may be contradictory and ambiguous but we know that that is the nature of our work. This is perhaps an unusual way of collating our data but it will serve as an informal reference for our work.

Who will make the first contribution? [Someone offers] Thank you.

The rest of you, choose a pen. There are many colours to choose from and this may be important to you. You may have to wait a moment for a space before you begin. [They begin]

As they are working,

Teacher: You may see a word or phrase that triggers another idea that you may want to add.

When everyone has contributed,

Teacher: It is important that we all have a chance to read what has been written. We are going to walk around this outline so that we all have the opportunity to see our collective impressions of this young boy.

As they are circling, it may be appropriate to ask participants to read aloud the words or phrases that stand out for them.

Teacher: Note any contradictions and ambiguities, anything that surprises you. [They respond]

Thank you. I will just hang this up here so that we can use it for our reference, should we need it.

As the teacher does so,

Teacher: It is, of course, the exposure to these differences that heightens our awareness of the possibilities that lie within this boy. Is he a poet or is he illiterate? Can he be both?

4. Giving Ben a background — ***10 minutes***

Grouping: **Individual**
Strategy: **Writing**
Administration: **Note cards; pencils and/or pens; masking tape**
Focus: **To provide a normal life for Ben**

Teacher: So, here we have Ben as we know him today. [*Teacher indicating the cut-out that s/he has put up on the wall*] But we also know that life for Ben had been different. He enjoyed blue skies, the parks and the streets of his city. He tells us he had a family and that he went to school. But that is all we know of his past. I wonder if I can ask you to use your own experiences of your childhood to help us fill in Ben's background? This is the kind of thing an actor would do to prepare for a role if that information were not available in the text.

As the teacher hands out the note cards,

While I am giving everyone a note card, think of a time in your childhood that stands out for you as a positive memory. It may be as simple as going to a fair or birthday party, picking fruit or sitting down to dinner with family; perhaps your first day at school. Remember these will be glimpses into Ben's life that will help us to understand him today.

You might want to begin with, "I'll never forget . . ." or "The sky was blue, the sun shining . . ." or "I remember so well when . . .".

I think five minutes should do it? Off you go. [They write]

Finish up what you are writing and we will hear some of these memories that we are giving to Ben. Who would like to share first? [They do]

I'll collect these to add to Ben's life.

We don't need to hear all of the students' memories but it would be helpful for later work if the teacher collected them and pinned around the Role on the Wall.

Are we ready to move on?

5. More about Ben's world ***3 minutes***

Grouping:	**Whole group**
Strategy:	**Reading a picture**
Administration:	**Picture (without the text) of the bicycle on pages four/five projected as an overhead or other media.**
Focus:	**To discover the world from Ben's window**

Teacher: Let's have a look at this picture. What do you see? [They say]

What is the mood? [They say]

In your mind's ear, what sounds do you hear? [They say]

As you continue to look at this picture, listen to the text that accompanies it.

Teacher reads from: ***I peers throo the kertins*** … to … ***But the seesons are topsee-turvee. Nothing is rite.***

6. Working as artists **5 minutes**

Grouping: **Groups of five**
Strategy: **Tableau**
Administration: **None**
Focus: **To interpret the picture kinesthetically**

Teacher: Get into groups of five, please. [They do]

Taking the essence of how you read the illustration, you are now going to respond as visual artists and, using your bodies, you will interpret the meaning of the picture as a tableau. Think of this as an abstract painting that might hang in a gallery dealing with contemporary issues. We are not expecting to see a re-creation of this illustration but, rather, your artistic interpretation of the mood generated by this picture.

Is everyone clear about the task?

Good, You only have three minutes to generate your response. Let's begin.

Teacher circulates to address any concerns and to encourage abstract interpretation. After about three minutes,

Teacher: Stop now. This is your chance to rehearse and to be sure that you know your place in this picture. I am going to count down from five and in that time, take your positions in the picture. By the time I am finished counting, you will be frozen in position. [*Teacher counts down*]

One person step out of the tableau now and, seeing as an artist, make any adjustments to the work that will help to engage and focus the observer's attention. [They do]

Observer, return to your place.

Remember where you are, as we will be coming back to these tableaux.

Relax everyone and take a moment to talk about any necessary shifts that were made. We'll see these as a gallery viewing without stopping. Who would like to go first? [They share]

Thank you.

What more do we now know about Ben's world? [They share]

7. Synthesizing words and picture ***10 minutes***

Grouping: **Groups (as above)**

Strategy: **Found poetry**

Administration: **Text of *Woolvs in the Sitee* (see Figure 7); one copy per student**

Focus: **To work with another form of interpretation**

Teacher: In the last strategy, we worked as artists. Now, I am going to ask you to work as poets. But as in any art form, there are constraints.

I will give you a copy of the text that accompanies the picture.

As poets, choose words and phrases from the text that as a group will serve to expand, through words, the essence of the tableau you have just created. Your found poem will be *four lines only.* This will require that you choose the words carefully and order them in a way that deepens our understanding of what we shall be seeing.

Use the blank part of the page to record your ideas. You are free to add three words of your own choosing, if you feel it necessary. You may write, using Ben's spelling or you may prefer to use standard spelling. [They write]

Now that you have composed your poem, you will need to practice how you will present it. You may want everyone in the group to speak all the lines; you may want certain lines or words said individually or by a pair. You may also want to pick up on the sounds that we have already identified and use them as accompaniment. As actors, of course, using all of your experience, your job is to interpret your text in such a way that the listeners will be invited into your meaning.

When the groups appear to be almost ready,

Teacher: Finish up now. [They do]

<u>***8. Building the context*** **10 minutes**</u>

Grouping:	**Groups of five (as above)**
Strategy:	**Montage**
Administration:	**Found poem texts**
Focus:	**To layer multiple interpretations to deepen meaning**

Teacher: Each group now has two different interpretations of the same picture—a tableau and a poem. We are now going to work with a theatrical strategy called *montage*. We use montage as a way of breaking up the expected in order to see our work from other perspectives. In this case, we will be sharing our poetry as a verbal contribution to *another* group's tableau. Any questions?

Try not to lose the rhythm of the lesson by getting hung up in a lot of questions when in actual fact those questions will be answered as they work.

Teacher: Good. We have the poems and we have the tableaux. We will present these as a film loop. We won't stop after each group has presented, but hear and see each group as part of a whole performance.

Each group, find your own space around the room. [They do]

Take a moment to recall your tableau positions. Do we need a quick rehearsal?

Let them rehearse if they need to do so. The teacher should know from their previous work if they really need a rehearsal.

Teacher: Where will we begin? [They decide] Good. Now, the group sitting to the right of this first group will be responsible for reading their poem to accompany the tableau. And so on around the circle.

Let's take a moment to figure out which group is speaking for whom. Got it? Good. Are we now ready to begin? [They agree]

After the sharing,

Teacher: Talk within your group about how the montage amplified or extended your work and your understanding of Ben's world. What new understandings did you gain? Thinking as an actor, what part of your experience helped you to situate yourself in this story? [They talk in their groups]

Depending on the conversations and the time, the teacher may want to open these conversations for whole class discussion. If time constraints are an issue, this reflection provides a natural break.

9. Meeting Missus Rudinski ***15 minutes***

Grouping: **Whole group/pairs**
Strategy: **Translating narration into dialogue**
Administration: **Text of *Woolvs in the Sitee* (see Figure 8)**
Focus: **To explore the central relationship of the story**

Teacher: In this next part of the drama, we are going to be working as actors. This next bit of text will give you the information you will need.

Teacher reads from: ***Sumtimes I opens the dor a chink*** … to … ***Missus Rudinski's veree kind, but she won't lissen abowt the woolvs.***

Teacher, handing out text and pencils,

Teacher: Here is the next part of the story, a meeting between Mrs. Rudinski and Ben. Read it silently to yourself and if you finish early, just think about what you have read. Don't talk about it yet. [They read silently]

Find a new partner and choose A and B. [They do]

Note: If there is a group of three, two of the students will take on the role of Ben. There is enough challenge here for this to happen productively.

Teacher: A will be Ben and B is Missus Rudinski. You will read this excerpt as dialogue from a scene in a play. That means we will hear not only the conversation already transcribed but you will have to change the inner thinking into dialogue. Who can give us an example of what we mean by that? [Someone volunteers]

Is everybody clear?

The challenge will be to improvise additional dialogue and blocking that makes this scene true for you.

After students have worked for about five minutes,

Teacher: A couple of things you might like to think about:

Where is the tension for Ben and how can you show that in your scene?

What might be Missus Rudinski's reasons for denying the wolves?

Talk about your relationship in terms of those questions and as you read through, use that new understanding to feed your interpretation. [They do]

Read again. When you have finished, talk about other ideas that might have occurred to you during this second reading. [They do]

I'm going to ask you now to get up and physicalize your ideas. Set your scene. How will you begin? How will you end? Let's take a little time to rehearse before we share. Remember we are still in the rehearsal process. This is not meant to be a final performance but in order for us to be able to move on, you need to have rehearsed.

When students appear to be ready (perhaps five minutes will be enough),

Teacher: Each pair, join with another. [They do]

Find a space in the room where you can work independently of the other groups. [They do]

In a moment, you are going to be sharing your scenes. As directors, what would we be looking for? [Class responds]

Good, now we have some valid criteria that will help us in our viewing.

Note: These scenes are shared between pairs, not presented to the whole group.

Before we begin, decide which pair will go first and set your scene. Some of you may prefer to work "off book" and improvise without reference to your scripts.

After each pair has shared, sit quietly and talk about your impressions.

Everyone ready? Take up your positions and then, take a moment to think in role.

When asking students to move into role, give them a few seconds to prepare, and when all are ready,

Teacher: And, begin.

After all scenes have been shared,

<u>**Teacher:**</u> Thank you. That was hard work. What do we now know that we didn't know before? What sorts of things have your inferred from this scene? Would anyone like to share their comments with the larger group? [They share]

Put your scripts away and find your own space where you will have room around you.

<u>10. What does Ben fear? 5 minutes</u>

Grouping: **Individual**

Strategy: **Movement**

Administration: **Music; we suggest Vaughan Williams' Symphony No. 7 *Sinfonia Antartica-Landscape***

Focus: **To embody the text**

<u>**Teacher:**</u> Everybody comfortable? [They nod] Are we ready to return to the text? Listen carefully.

<u>**Teacher reads from:**</u> ***Erly won morning, wen I'm squinching owt the window*** … to … ***I cannot moov. I shuts my eyes.***

Close your eyes and listen now to this piece of music. As you listen, visualize in your mind's eye what it is that is happening around Ben that causes him to be unable to move. [They listen as music plays]

After about a minute of music and now layering the reading over the music,

<u>**Teacher re-reads the text from:**</u> ***but it is not a reel sky*** … to … ***I cannot move, I shuts my eyes.***

From where you are, let the music help you to interpret through your movement what it is that so terrifies Ben.

Use the space available so that you can really become that terrifying thing that surrounds Ben. You may want to use sound to extend your imaginings. And, begin. [They do]

This is a preliminary movement experience that can easily be extended into a dance drama, depending upon the interest of your students. Some may want to work on this as a small group for presentation to the rest of the class or the whole class may want to choreograph the piece (see Brian Way, 1967, chapter 5).

Teacher: Just talk to the people around you about the images or sounds that motivated the movement. Share what you imagined it was that so terrified Ben.

Who would like to share with the rest of us? [They share]

Thank you. Let's move on.

11. More of the story ***5 minutes***

Grouping: **Whole class**
Strategy: **Reading and listening**
Administration: **Text of *Woolvs in the Sitee***
Focus: **To build our knowledge of Ben**

Teacher reads from: ***The wall is starting to darken*** … (*this repeat is necessary for continuation*) to the end of the story.

12. Writing on walls ***10 minutes***

Grouping: **Whole class**
Strategy: **Graffiti**
Administration: **Long roll of paper; lots of felt pens with good strong colours**
Focus: **To give voice to Ben**

<u>**Teacher:**</u> Ben has broken free and invites others to join him. As Ben, what sorts of things would you write on the walls of the city to encourage the community to take a stand, to live under a blue sky and in a green land?

Give students enough time to generate the wall.

<u>**Teacher:**</u> Finish up your writing, Ben. Thank you.

Find someone to talk with as you read the messages that Ben has left. Think about who might read them and how they might respond. [They do]

13. Making a visible choice ***7 minutes***

Grouping: **Individuals**
Strategy: **Spectrum of difference**
Administration: **Space large enough for every student to stand in a line**
Focus: **To commit by taking a position**

<u>**Teacher:**</u> Now comes what may be for you the most challenging action of this drama. In role as a member of this community, think about a word or phrase that most clearly reflects where you, yourself, stand in response to Ben's call. You may use your own words or something that you've read that speaks more directly to what you are thinking and feeling.

As you make this choice, you need to think very carefully about what is happening in the city around you. Where do the dangers lie? What may be the consequences of joining Ben? How might your choice affect your family? Your own career? And the safety of those you love?

Consider carefully what you are prepared to do, what you may lose and what you may or may not gain by joining Ben. Again, no need to feel rushed. We have time.

After enough time for deciding,

Teacher: Let that choice inform what will happen next. Please come over here [*Indicating a clear space*] and just listen for a moment.

Teacher: Is there someone who is willing to stand shoulder to shoulder with Ben? [Someone volunteers]

Please come and stand over here. [*Indicates the front of the line*] Thank you.

Teacher to the group: Keeping the words you have chosen in mind, I am going to ask you to place yourself in relation to [*Name of student*] along this continuum. [*Indicates the imaginary line*]

Note: There must be enough space for all students to find their places on the line.

Teacher: As you find your place, consider how much of a risk you are willing to take in response to what is happening around you. Some of you may feel strongly about what is happening, some afraid. Some of you may feel this is not the right time to speak out. Some of you see what is happening but accept that this is just the way things unfold.

As one of those who has read Ben's call and considering your view of the world at this particular time, place yourself on this imaginary line to indicate where you stand in relation to Ben and [*Names student*]. Are you close to their thinking? Or do you stand somewhere further away? Work silently.

Allow students to organize themselves on the continuum.

Teacher: The risk of speaking out for some people may be greater than for others but we need to be sure that all voices are heard. From which end shall we begin? [They choose]

Close your eyes and let's hear those words from the wall. When you are ready, begin. [They speak]

Thank you. Sit down and talk to the people around you about the choice you made. On the basis of what we have heard, what have we learned about this community? How might that account for the situation in which we found Ben at the beginning of the story? [They talk]

Let's share some of those conversations you have just had. [They share]

14. Reflection and connection — ***As long as needed***

Grouping: **As above**
Strategy: **Reflection**
Administration: **Role on the wall; note cards (from activities 4 and 5)**
Focus: **To try and understand what gave Ben courage**

Teacher: We have worked long and hard to understand the life of a child named Ben. Let's look back on how we first saw him and some of the words we used to describe him. Is there anything that might give us some indication, some glimmer of the extraordinary transformation that caused him to leave the shelter of his room and go out to search for Missus Rudinski?

This question might also be appropriate:

We have access to a great deal of information about our larger world. I am wondering what connections you can make between this story and what is happening (or has happened) in other countries or right here at home, where children appear to have been abandoned?

The teacher might want to bring in relevant material from newspapers, journals and so on.

Although this is a fictional story, you all were prepared to put yourselves somewhere on the line. In real life people are doing this all the time, all over the world. What examples can you think of?

The teacher may feel that a stronger prompt is appropriate.

Perhaps you may have heard of the young student who put himself in front of the tank in Tiananmen Square or the young couple from different sides of the Bosnian war who had the courage to follow their hearts, or of the people who chose to hide others during the Second World War. There are many examples nearer our own time. I am thinking of the passengers on the flight hijacked by terrorists, those who chose to take a stand as the plane was headed towards the White House. Of course, those are life and death choices. But they were all ordinary people who found themselves in extraordinary situations.

I am wondering what motivates people to make these choices?

Where do we see those qualities in Ben? He was just a regular kid and we know he was very frightened by his world.

Extension

Students may be intrigued by the story and want to write their own versions of what they understand to have happened to Ben's world. They may choose to do it from an historical perspective of 50 years in the future. In that case, what role perspective might they take on? What do they remember of that time? How have things changed and how have those changes affected the world?

Materials

Activity 1: An old bag; tins of food; matches; flashlight; an old woman's sweater; a note: ***Ive gon looking for yoo. Yor frend, Ben***
Activity 2: Text of *Woolvs in the Sitee* (pages one and two, see Figure 6)
Activity 3: Life-size cut-out of young boy; felt pens
Activity 4: Note cards and pencils/pens; masking tape
Activity 5: Picture of the bicycle on pages four/five, no text, to be projected as an overhead or other media
Activity 7: Text of *Woolvs in the Sitee* (see Figure 7), one copy per student
Activity 8: Found poem texts
Activity 9: Text of *Woolvs in the Sitee* (see Figure 8)
Activity 10: Music
Activity 11: Text of *Woolvs in the Sitee*
Activity 12: Long roll of paper; brightly coloured felt pens for all
Activity 14: Role on the wall; note cards (from Activities 4 and 5)

Resources

Way, B. (1967). *Development through drama*. London: Longman.
Wild, M., & Spudvilas, A. (2007). *Woolvs in the sitee*. Asheville, NC: Front Street.

There are woolvs in the sitee. Oh, yes!
In the streets, in the parks, in the allees.
In shops, in rustee playgrownds,
in howses rite next dor

And soon they will kum.
They will kum for me and for yoo
and for yor bruthers and sisters,
yor mothers and fathers, yor arnts and
yor grandfathers and grandmothers.

No won is spared.

Lissen to me.
Lissen!

I yoosed to hav a familee, a home.
These streets wer my rivers,
these parks my vallees.

Now I am scrooched up in won room
in a mustee basement, heavy kertins across
the window.

Figure 6: Text for Activity 2. May be photocopied for classroom use. © 2016 *Into the Story 2: More Stories! More Drama!* by Carole Miller and Juliana Saxton. Bristol, UK: Intellect.

I peers throo the kertins, I peers at the stranj, streekee sunsets.

The sitee is hush, the traffik long-
ago gone. Onlee now and agen do
I heer the swish of a bisikil.

I don't need to sqint owt the
window to no that the rider
is glansing over his sholder,
terrified.

I longs for bloo skys.
I longs for it to rane.
But the seasons are topsee-turvee.

Nothing is rite.

Figure 7: Text for Activity 7. May be photocopied for classroom use. © 2016 *Into the Story 2: More Stories! More Drama!* by Carole Miller and Juliana Saxton. Bristol, UK: Intellect.

Sumtimes I opens the dor a chink.
Then I creeps up the stares to ask my naybor
if she can spare sum water.

Missus Rudinski's veree kind, but she
won't lissen abowt the woolvs.

"Yoo need to get owt more," she sez.
"Go bak to skool, take up a hobbee."

She dusn't unnerstand abowt the woolvs.
She thinks I'm torking abowt those luvlee
wyld creechis, running in the woods.
That's not wot I meens.

Not at all!

These woolvs are hatefuls,
and hating.
They are in the sitee,
they are evereewhere.

They spare no won.

Lissen.
Lissen,
Missus
Rudinski!
. . .
But she sez, "Why do yoo call them
woolvs, Ben? Yoo no that can't be."

"Can't it?" I say. "Yoo must hav seen
there shadows, Missus. Yoo must hav!"

"No," she sez. "I haven't seen anee shadows."

But I no she has. She has
seen those shadows prowling along
pavments, snarling up walls.

That's why she stares up at the
sky wen she goes serching for
water with her littil buket
She offen trips. Grazes an elbow,
a nee. I don't blame her for not
looking down.

Figure 8: Text for Activity 9. May be photocopied for classroom use. © 2016 *Into the Story 2: More Stories! More Drama!* by Carole Miller and Juliana Saxton. Bristol, UK: Intellect.

Recommended Reading

Ackroyd, J. and Boulton, J. (2013a). *Drama lessons: Ages 7–11* (2nd ed.). New York, NY: Routledge.

Ackroyd, J. and Boulton, J. (2013b). *Drama lessons: Ages 4–7* (2nd ed.). New York, NY: Routledge.

Anderson, M., Hughes, J. and Manuel, J. (Eds.). (2008). *Drama in English teaching: Imagination, action and engagement*. Oxford, UK: Oxford University Press.

Baldwin, P. (2004/2012). *With drama in mind: Real learning in imagined worlds* (2nd ed.). New York, NY: Continuum.

Baldwin, P. and John, R. (2012). *Inspiring writing through drama: Creative approaches to teaching ages 7–16*. New York, NY: Bloomsbury Education.

Barrs, M., Barton, B. and Booth, D. (2012). *This book is not about drama ... it's about new ways to inspire students*. Markham, ON: Pembroke Publishers.

Belliveau, G. (2014). *Stepping into drama:* A Midsummer Night's Dream *in the elementary classroom*. Vancouver, BC: Pacific Educational Press

Booth, D. and Hachiya, M. (2004). *Arts go to school*. Markham, ON: Pembroke Publishers.

Booth, D. (2005). *Story drama: Creating stories through role playing, improvising and reading aloud* (2nd ed.). Markham, ON: Pembroke Publishers.

Booth, D. (2014). *Exploding the reading: Building a world of responses from one story*. Markham, ON: Pembroke Publishers.

Bowell, P. and Heap, B. (2013). *Planning process drama: Enriching teaching and learning* (2nd ed.). New York, NY: Routledge.

Carleton, J. P. (2012). *Story drama in the special needs classroom: Step-by-step lesson plans for teaching through dramatic play*. London, UK: Jessica Kingsley.

Doona, J. (2014). *Secondary drama: A creative source book: Practical inspiration for teachers*. Milton Park, Abingdon, Oxon: Routledge.

Ewing, R. (2013). *Creative arts in the lives of young children: Play, imagination and learning*. Melbourne: ACER Press.

Hulson, M. (2006). *Schemes for classroom drama*. Stoke on Trent, UK: Trentham Books.

Lundy, K. (2014). *Teaching fairly in an unfair world*. Markham, ON: Pembroke Publishers.

Lundy, K. and Swartz, L. (2011). *Creating caring classrooms: How to encourage students to communicate, create, and be compassionate of others*. Markham, ON: Pembroke Publishers.

Miller, C. and Saxton, J. (2004). *Into the story: Language in action through drama*. Portsmouth, NH: Heinemann.

Neelands, J. and Goode, T. (2000). *Structuring drama work* (2nd ed.). Cambridge, UK: Cambridge University Press.

Prendergast, M. and Saxton, J. (2013). *Applied drama: A facilitator's handbook for working in community*. Bristol, UK: Intellect.

Rainer, J. and Lewis, M. (2012). *Drama at the heart of the secondary school: Projects to promote authentic learning*. New York, NY: Routledge.

Swartz, L. (2014). *Dramathemes* (4th ed.). Markham, ON: Pembroke Publishers.

Swartz, L. and Nyman, D. (2010). *Drama schemes, themes & dreams: How to plan, structure, and assess classroom events that engage all learners*. Markham, ON: Pembroke Publishers.

Web resources

Farmer, D. (2013, February 3). KS 1/2 Drama: A workshop with Cecily O'Neill. Retrieved from http://www.youtube.com. One of our great UK drama educators at work.

O'Connor, P. (2012, April 26). A teaspoon of light: Full performance. Retrieved from http://www.youtube.com. This is the full process drama based on Dr O'Connor's work after the Christchurch, NZ earthquake.

Bibliography

Amato, E. (2007). *Tricycle.* Toronto, ON: Groundwood Books/House of Anansi Press.

Baldwin, P. (2012). *With drama in mind: Real learning in imagined worlds.* London: Bloomsbury.

Baron Cohen, S. (2001). Theory of mind in normal development and autism. *Prisme, 34,* 174–183. Retrieved from www.autism-community.com/wp-content/.../TOM-in-TD-and-ASD.pdf

Beckerman, B. (1970). *The dynamics of drama: Theory and method of analysis.* New York, NY: Alfred A Knopf.

Bloem, P., Kloostser, D. and Preece, A. (2008). Many voices in the classroom: The role of classroom talk in education for democracy. *Thinking Classroom, 9*(4), 6–18.

Boal, A. (2002). *Games for actors and non-actors* (A. Jackson, Trans.). New York, NY: Routledge

Booth, D. (2014, December). Book of the month preview: An interview with David Booth. *Pembroke E-News* (December). Retrieved from www.pembrokepublishers.com

Booth, D. and Neelands, J. (Eds.). (1998). *Writing in-role.* Hamilton, ON: Caliburn Enterprises.

Boelts, M. (2007). *Those shoes.* Somerville, MA: Candlewick Press.

Bolton, G. (2003). *Dorothy Heathcote's story: Biography of a remarkable drama teacher.* Stoke on Trent, UK: Trentham Books.

Bruner, J. (1986). *Actual minds, possible worlds.* Cambridge, MA: Harvard University Press.

Buber, M. (1965). *Between man and man* (R. G. Smith, Trans.). New York, NY: Macmillan Publishing.

Chambers, A. (1985). *Booktalk*. Stroud, UK: Thimble Press.

Chanowitz, B. and Langer, E. (1981). Premature cognitive commitment. *Journal of Personality and Social Psychology, 41,* 1051–1063.

Crew. G. (2004). *Beneath the surface.* Sydney, AU: Hodder Children's Books.

Crumpler, T. and Schneider, J. (2002). Writing with their whole being: A cross study analysis of children's writing from five classrooms using process drama. *Research in Drama Education,* 7(2), 61–79.

Djikic, M., Oatley, K., Zoeterman, S. and Peterson, J. (2009). On being moved by art: How reading fiction transforms the self. *Creativity Research Journal, 21*(1), 24–29.

Eliot, T. S. (1968). *Old possum's book of practical cats.* New York, NY: Mariner Books.

Ewing, R. (2010). The arts and Australian education: Realizing potential. *Australian Education Review, 58.* Camberwell, VIC: The Australian Council for Educational Research.

Fox, M. (1984). *Wilfrid Gordon McDonald Partridge.* Toronto, ON: Puffin/Penguin Books.

Fox, M. (2006). *Fox.* St. Louis, MO: Turtleback Books.

Goldstein, T., Wu, K. and Winner, E. (2009). Actors are skilled in theory of mind but not empathy. *Imagination, Cognition and Personality, 29*(2), 115–133.

Goleman, D. (2006). *Social intelligence: The new science of human relationships.* New York, NY: Bantam Books.

Greene, M. (1995). *Releasing the imagination: Essays on education, the arts and social change.* San Francisco, CA: Jossey-Bass.

Heath, S. B. (2000). Seeing our way into learning. *Cambridge Journal of Education, 30*(1), 121–131.

Heathcote, D. and Bolton, G. (1995). *Drama for learning: Dorothy Heathcote's mantle of the expert approach to education.* London, UK: Pearson Education Books.

Hirsh-Pasek, K. and Golinkoff, R. M. (2003). *Einstein never used flash cards: How our children really learn – and why they need to play more and memorize less.* Emmaus, PA: Rodale.

Innocenti, R., and Gallaz, C. (1985). *Rose Blanche.* Mankato, MN: The Creative Company.

Johnson, L. and O'Neill, C. (1984). *Dorothy Heathcote: Collected writings on education and drama.* London: Hutchinson Education.

Kennedy, R. F. (1968). Recapturing America's moral vision. In *RFK: Collected speeches* (pp. 329–330). New York, NY: Viking Penguin .

Krznaric, R. (2014). *A handbook for revolution: Empathy.* London, UK: Routledge.

Langer, E. and Piper, J. (1987). The prevention of mindlessness. *Journal of Personality and Social Psychology, 53*(2), 280–287.

Langer, E., Hatem, M., Joss, J. and Howell, M. (1989). The role of uncertainty in education. *Creativity Research Journal, 2*(3), 139–150.

Mar, R., Oatley, K., Hirsh, J., dela Paz, J. and Peterson, J. (2006). Book worms versus nerds: Exposure to fiction versus non-fiction, divergent associations with social ability, and the simulation of fictional social worlds. *ScienceDirect, Journal of Research in Personality, 40,* 694–712.

Miller, C. and Saxton, J. (2004). *Into the story: Language in action through drama.* Portsmouth, NH: Heinemann.

Morgan, N. and Saxton, J. (2006). *Asking better questions* (2nd ed.). Markham, ON: Pembroke.

Neelands, J. (1984). *Making sense of drama.* London, UK: Heinemann.

Neelands, J. (2006). The idea of IDEA is a people's theatre. In L. McCammon and D. McLauchlan (Eds.), *Universal mosaic of drama and theatre: The IDEA 2004 dialogues* (pp. 55–63). Ottawa, ON: IDEA Publications.

Neelands, J. (2010). 11/09 – The space in our hearts. In P. O'Connor (Ed.), *Creating democratic citizenship through drama education: The writings of Jonothan Neelands* (pp. 119–129). Stoke on Trent, UK: Trentham Books.

O'Connor, P. (2012). Tribute. In J. Saxton and C. Miller (Eds.), Points and practices: In memory of Dorothy Heathcote, MBE (pp. 7–34). *RiDE: The Journal of Applied Theatre and Performance, 17*(1), 22.

O'Mara, J. (2004). At Sunny Bay: Building students' repertoire of literacy practices through process drama. In A. Healy and E. Honan (Eds.), *Text next: New resources for literacy learning* (pp. 119–136). Sydney, NSW: Primary English Teaching Association.

O'Mara, J. (2008). Reading and writing ourselves into the 21st century. In M. Anderson, J. Hughes and J. Manuel (Eds.), *Drama in English teaching: Imagination, action and engagement.* Oxford, UK: Oxford University Press.

Opie, I. and P. (1969). *Children's games in street and playground.* Oxford, UK: Oxford University Press.

O'Toole, J. (2015). Teaching by terror: Ordeal, ego and education. In P. Duffy (Ed.), *A reflective practitioner's guide to (mis)adventures in drama education – or – What was I thinking?* (pp. 115–129). Bristol, UK: Intellect.

O'Toole, J. and Dunn, J. (2002). *Pretending to learn: Helping children learn through drama.* Frenchs Forest, NSW: Pearson Education Australia.

Pianta, R., Belsky, J., Houts, R. and Morrison, F. (2007). Opportunities to learn in America's elementary classrooms. *Science, 315,* 1795–1796.

Robinson, K. (2009). *The element: How finding your passion changes everything.* New York, NY: Penguin.

Safford, K. and Barrs, M. (2005). *Many routes to meaning: Children's language and literacy development in creative arts work.* London: Centre for Literacy in Primary Education. Retrieved from http://www.clpe.co.uk/pdf/many_routes_to_meaning.pdf.

Sennett, R. (2012). *Together: The rituals, pleasures and politics of cooperation.* New Haven, CT: Yale University Press.

Siegel, D. (2007). *The mindful brain: Reflection and attunement in the cultivation of well-being.* New York, NY: WW Norton & Co.

Sinclair, C., Donelan, K., Bird, J., O'Toole, J. and Freebody, K. (2009). Drama: Social dreaming in the twenty-first century. In C. Sinclair, N. Jeanneret and J. O'Toole (Eds.), *Education in the arts.* Melbourne, AU: Oxford University Press.

Skármeta, A. (2000). *The composition* (E. Amato, Trans.). Toronto, ON: Groundwood Books/House of Anansi Press.

Thompson, R. (2000). *The follower.* Toronto, ON: Fitzhenry & Whiteside.
UNESCO Joint Declaration of the International Drama/Theatre and Education Association (IDEA), International Society for Education through Art (InSEA), International Society for Music Education (ISME) (2007). Viseu, Portugal. Retrieved from http://www.assitej.org/doc/Joint%20Declaration.pdf.
Watts, I. (1996). *The fish princess.* Toronto, ON: Tundra Books.
Way, B. (1967). *Development through drama.* London: Longman.
Wild, M. and Spudvilas, A. (2007). *Woolvs in the sitee.* Asheville, NC: Front Street.
Winner, E., Goldstein, T. R. and Vincent-Lancrin, S. (2013). *Art for art's sake?: The impact of arts education.* Paris: OECD Centre for Educational Research and Innovation.
Wojciehowski, H. and Gallese, V. (2011). How stories make us feel: Toward an embodied narratology. *Journal of California Italian Studies, 2*(1), 1–35.
Wolk, S. (2008). School as inquiry. *Phi Delta Kappan, 90*(2), 115–122.
Woodruff, P. (2008). *The necessity of theater: The art of watching and being watched.* New York, NY: Oxford University Press.

Glossary of Drama Strategies

There are a number of strategies listed in these story drama structures that are familiar to all teachers: brainstorming, listening, designing, discussion, drawing, mapping, movement, planning, predicting, puzzles, reading aloud, silent follow-along and storytelling. Although they may appear in the structures, we do not list them. The following strategies have a particular or significant use for the story drama structures.

We have tried to include the explanation of each strategy within the teacher talk of the structures. However, when a strategy is new to the group, it may need to be explained in more detail, demonstrated or practiced. As participants become more experienced, they may need only a reminder of what the terms mean.

Building an image Teacher or a participant acts as a blank canvas upon which the rest of the group can "draw" their ideas. Participants respond to the invitation to create an image by making suggestions or physically adjusting the body of the person as if it were "clay". The teacher or participant may ask questions; for example, "Is this how you want me to hold my arm?" or, "Where should I focus my eyes?" A participant or participants may then join the original image, adding or responding to the idea/s so that the perspectives are enlarged.

Building lists List building is a useful, non-judgmental way in which to discover and share what is in the minds of individuals and the collective understanding of the group.

Building questions While information gathering is important, the value of questions is to inquire into thinking, attitudes and motivations of self and others. This is a useful strategy to prepare participants for an improvisation or a hot seating activity. Participants learn to ask and suggest answers to open-ended questions.

Captioning Captioning expresses meaning in written form through a succinct statement that underscores what is being presented visually. Captioning may also be referred to as headlines or titles.

Conscience alley The participants form two lines facing each other. The person who has made or must make a decision or has something on his or her mind walks slowly between. As he or she moves down the line, the pair on either side comment or reflect (either as themselves or in role) on the difficulty or choice. The lines act as a collective conscience and they may give the character advice based on moral or political choices. Another use for conscience alley is to express the thinking or feeling of the character who is moving down the line.

Drama contract Integral to effective drama practice is the drama contract, whether explicit or implied. Even though the students will be inside the drama fiction, regular classroom behaviour is expected; for example: working well in a group, accepting the "as if" world of the drama; respecting each other's space and opinions in role and so on. This contract will be familiar as most classrooms negotiate the rules at the very beginning of the year. These rules may be added to as the students become more experienced (see Neelands, 1984).

Exercise A drama exercise may be done individually or in a variety of groupings for the purpose of developing a skill or to set the context for the work. It is short-term and has a specific goal or stopping point. Exercise is initiated with instructions, the rules are clear and an exercise is easily repeatable.

Found poetry Found poetry is created by using the words and images in a text to create a new text that layers in the participants' own thoughts and feelings.

Game Games develop group skills and help participants to discover how rules make things work; they are useful diagnostic devices for assessing group health. In these story drama structures, we use games as metaphors or symbolic ways to frame the story. Iona and Peter Opie in *Children's Games in Street and Playground* (1969) remind us that all games are analogies for human situations.

Gossip mill This is a useful way to generate background information or rumours about the situation being played. The participants are asked to think about one reason that caused the situation or to share a memory of an event. They mill about stopping on a signal, to share their information with another participant. This may be done a number of times so that the rumours flow. Older students may not need the signal and can mill about with less structure. The gossip should be shared, valued or discounted with the entire group in reflection.

Guided imagery This strategy is used when it is important that everyone can visualize the same situation at the same time.

Hot seating Hot seating is used when participants have a need to expand their understanding by questioning a character in role. Participants may or may not be in role, but the questions are ones that need to be asked, and therefore, it is often useful to prepare at least some in advance. The teacher may be the person in the hot seat. When using students in hot seating it is often safer for them if they can share the role. This provides opportunities for hearing different perspectives. The task is to listen very carefully to each other and build on what they have heard and not contradict what has already been said.

Improvisation Improvisation is the basic communicative form for many of the strategies in this glossary. When we improvise, we are moving, thinking and talking spontaneously, in response to what is happening.

Mantle of the expert Participants are endowed with a special expertise in order to accomplish the work. This task-driven activity should be done seriously and with great attention as participants look at the situation through "special" eyes and bring their "expert" understanding and skills into play. It's a wonderful opportunity to elevate students' thinking, language and presence. Mantle of the expert as a teaching *pedagogy* may be found in Heathcote and Bolton's (1995) *Drama for Learning*.

Montage Montage is a means of layering two different strategies based on the interpretation of the same experience. It allows us to see the work through different lenses as another way to amplify meaning.

Narration Narration is used to link one activity to another and is necessary for coherence. It serves to tell of the events that happened in between activities that will not be experienced by the participants. Narration requires the skills of the storyteller in order to heighten the significance of events and to provide an affective resonance to them.

Presenting The focus of presenting is on the process of making. Presentations are not meant to be valued for their polish but for what they contribute to our understanding.

Reading a picture Participants make meaning from illustrations that introduce them to themes, characters, settings and the affective context of stories. Participants' experiences, knowledge and values are brought to the reading and are shared collectively through their responses. It is an effective way of introducing the subtleties of signs.

Re-enactment The re-creation of the actions in the text is referred to as re-enactment. Re-enacting can be done as the text is being read or following the reading. During a reading, participants are able to connect with the affective context. When used following the reading, participants are much more engaged in remembering the sequence of events. In both, there is an emphasis on accuracy of detail and making the drama real.

Reflection Reflection helps the participants stand back from the drama and to consolidate the meanings and/or issues that are emerging. Reflection is also a means of reviewing and commenting on the action. Reflection not only happens at the end of the drama experience as a way of moving away from the fictional world, but it also occurs both in role and out of role. There are many strategies that encourage reflection because it is a significant means by which participants may bring their own thoughts and feelings into their understanding of the drama, themselves and others.

Ritual This strategy slows down and elevates the significance of the action. It is a powerful means for moving participants more deeply into the drama because it enables them to recognize the importance of their actions.

Role Working in role is foundational to drama. It is the means by which participants enter into the world of pretend, something that all children can do very well. To be in role means to assume the attitudes and points of view of a fictitious person. The skills demanded by role-playing are simply those of thinking "as if I were walking in someone else's shoes". The only rule for role-playing is that what is said and done in role must be true to the context. When participants are working in role, they are protected by the role and therefore able to express themselves in ways that may be different from their own realities.

Role on the wall Life-size blank cut-outs or outlines drawn on the board may be used to build background by having participants write words or phrases that describe the character and/or thoughts and feelings of the character. These figures may be returned to and/or words added to as a means of reflecting new understanding.

Sculpting or moulding As in Building an image, one person shapes someone (usually a partner) into a figure that represents the sculptor's image or perception of that image. The partner acts as "clay" and responds to the touch or direction of his or her partner. The less talking there is, the better. This strategy involves trust; participants need to be reminded to respect their partners and their ability to be shaped.

Soundscape This is a free-form composition using any arrangement of sounds and any combination of traditional instruments, non-traditional instruments, found objects, voices (words or sounds) and body percussion. It creates a picture in sound of a particular location, mood or dramatic setting.

Spectrum of difference Participants commit to an issue by taking a position on an imaginary line along a continuum that represents a scale from agreement to disagreement. This embodied action is an example of reflection in role and is a powerful means of developing critical literacy.

Tableau (also known as **Depiction** or **Still image**) Tableau is a frozen, three-dimensional picture of a person or group of people, representing their understanding of a particular context. Although it may be abstract, it represents concretized thinking. Sometimes it is enough just to see a tableau; sometimes you may want to focus the observations by asking, "What do we see?" or by tapping in: "To whom shall we speak?" "What question shall we ask?" This strategy is useful for developing participants' presentational skills as well as audience skills. It is a powerful way to work in drama and is low-risk for both participants and facilitator.

Tapping in Participants are frozen (in tableaux) or sitting or standing still, often with their eyes closed. The teacher moves through the group placing a hand on each participant's shoulder and asking a question such as, "Tell us what you are thinking." "What are your concerns?" Keep your hand, gently but firmly, on the participant's shoulder until you are sure his or her statement has been completed. Sometimes participants are not prepared to speak; leave your hand in place until this is clear and then move on without comment. After modeling, students may choose to tap in.

Teacher in role The teacher takes part in the drama as a way of facilitating the learning from inside the story. Teacher in role enables the shift of responsibility for discovery from the teacher to the participants. It allows the teacher to be in control without being didactic. The role must guide the responses demanded by the role, not by the individual who inhabits it.

Teacher in fringe role Sometimes teacher in role will play a specific character in the story. Other times, teacher in role is just one of the crowd, not necessarily identifiable but someone who has the right to be there. For example, teacher may participate inside the drama as a means of moving the drama along. Remember, you are not "the teacher" but one of the group with no greater status than anyone else.

Transformation Participants create two images representing an experience in two difference circumstances; for example, a group of people in different time frames. In slow motion, the group transforms through movement from one image to the other (and, sometimes, back again). It is a way of exploring shifting perspectives. Transformation can also be used to shift from one character to another; for example, from a wolf to a knight (see *Into the story*, 2004, pp. 73–75).

Voice collage Participants speak aloud a phrase or sentence from a piece of writing (in or out of role). The teacher can control the collage by tapping in, or participants may speak aloud as they feel their phrases or sentences fit. You may find it useful to determine with the group who has the first line and you need to be sensitive as to when the collage is finished. Generally, "thank you" indicates that the collage is concluded. Voice collages are often used to create a mood or to let participants hear what other members of the group are thinking.

Writing in role This strategy is used as a means of reflecting inside the drama. The writing is always purposeful whether it is recording personal thoughts in a diary, appealing to a greater authority through a petition, communicating with a friend or administrator by letter or making information available through a newspaper article. The context of the drama provides the motivation for all kinds of writing that may be used in a variety of ways.

This glossary is adapted and extended from pp. 156 to 160 of *Into the story: Language in action through drama* (2004). We also draw on the work of John O'Toole and Julie Dunn (2002) and Jonothan Neelands (1990).

Appendix

Making a Story Drama Structure

Here are some ideas that may help you to look at the text and the illustrations from a variety of viewpoints. You can find your own order; not each idea needs to be considered.

Choosing a picture book

Find a story that you enjoy and to which you can relate.
Read the story a number of times.
What sorts of things do you begin to notice as you read?
What words/phrases are new to you?
What possibilities are there for language development? For example, Margaret Wild's (2006) *Fox* uses many words and phrases to describe speed.
What colours are used in the story? In the illustrations?
What smells, tastes, sounds are described?
What sort of music comes to mind?
What feelings/mood/s does the text generate; do the illustrations generate?
What images stay with you after reading the story?
What influences do the illustrations have on the movie in your head?
What is the plot of the story?
What curriculum needs does the story meet?
What life experiences do you have that are reflected by this story?
What are the big ideas embedded in this story; what could this story really be about? (Key understandings and questions)
Where might your students' experiences be matched to the story?

Designing the structure

What parts of the text lend themselves to drama activities?

What would be the focus of those activities?

Divide the story into its scenes. In a story drama structure these are described as activities that may be titled.

Consider how you will link one activity to the next so that the students know where they are, where they have come from and where they may be going.

Consider the following: Size of group; strategy; what you need to make the strategy happen? (Administration) and why you are doing this particular activity in this way? (Focus).

Who in the story might the students talk to? How might that be done?

What bits of the story will you read?

What parts of the story may need to be narrated?

When planning a story drama structure, try to hear in your head how what the words you are *saying* will effect what the students *do*. Often when you do that, you discover that instead of pairs, you should be using groups of four! Work for fewer words, clearer words and words that engage and intrigue your students into exploring and discovering meanings, meanings that you want them to discover and meanings that you have never thought of that they will tell you about.

Which pictures might you chose to show and why?

Would those pictures best be delivered by overhead/power point/data projector to the class, or given to each individual or to each group?

What reflection questions might you use to debrief the experiences? In role? Out of role?

What questions are there to be asked that will help make links between activities *and* with the big ideas? Remember, with each activity and its reflection you are creating, through meaning-making, the dramatic action (Beckerman, 1970) that carries the "play" and its participants towards understanding. Hopefully, these understandings will in some way help to connect each student to the ideas in the structure and by doing so, develop his or her worldview.

Post-teaching reflection

Remember that each time you do any story drama structure, it will be different.

Be sure to record any idea that worked better than the ones you did or you thought you might do.

Record all the good questions that arose in the reflective conversations—your own and those of your students.

Finally, sometimes you can find a great story and not have a clue how to use it. This happened to us with *Woolvs in the Sitee*. It took us more than a year of thinking … putting aside … thinking … to find the way in. If this happens to you, just put the story away for now and find another.

Enjoy!

Index

Note: Bold page numbers refer to glossary entries.